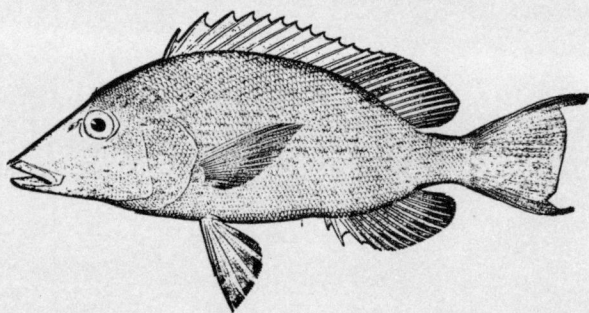

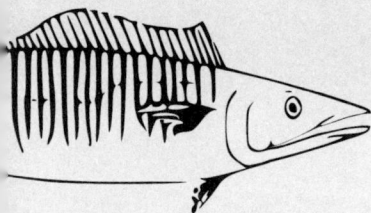

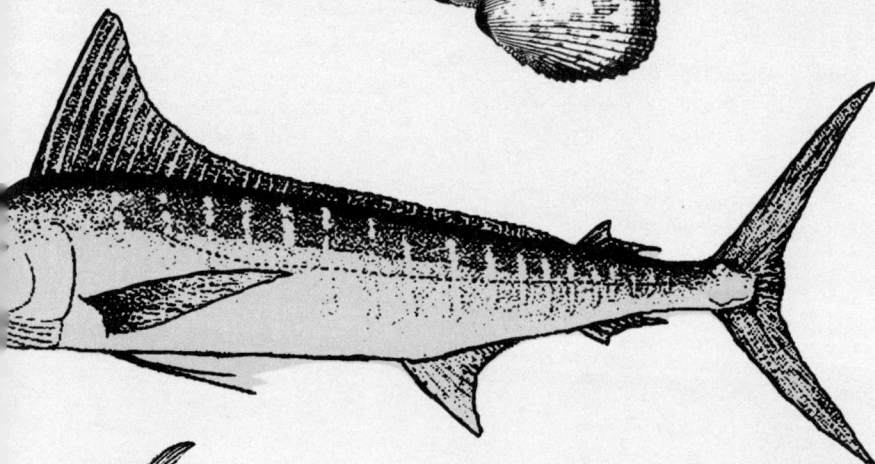

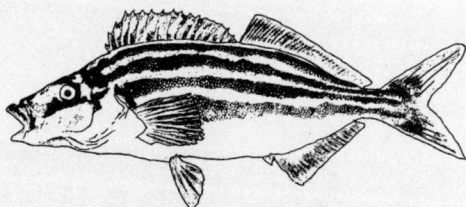
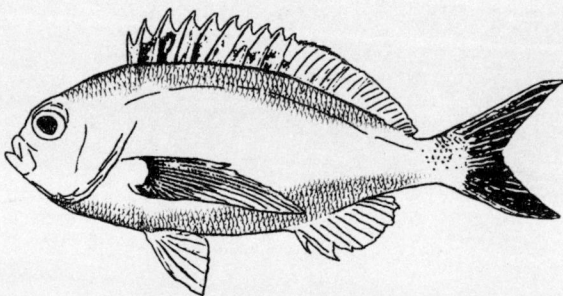
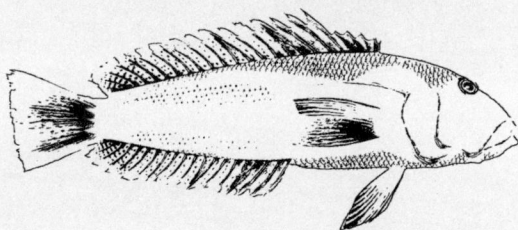
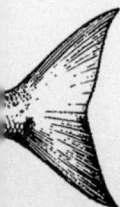

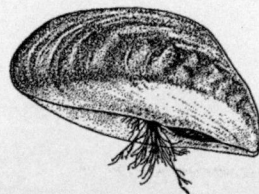

FISH
OF THE DAY

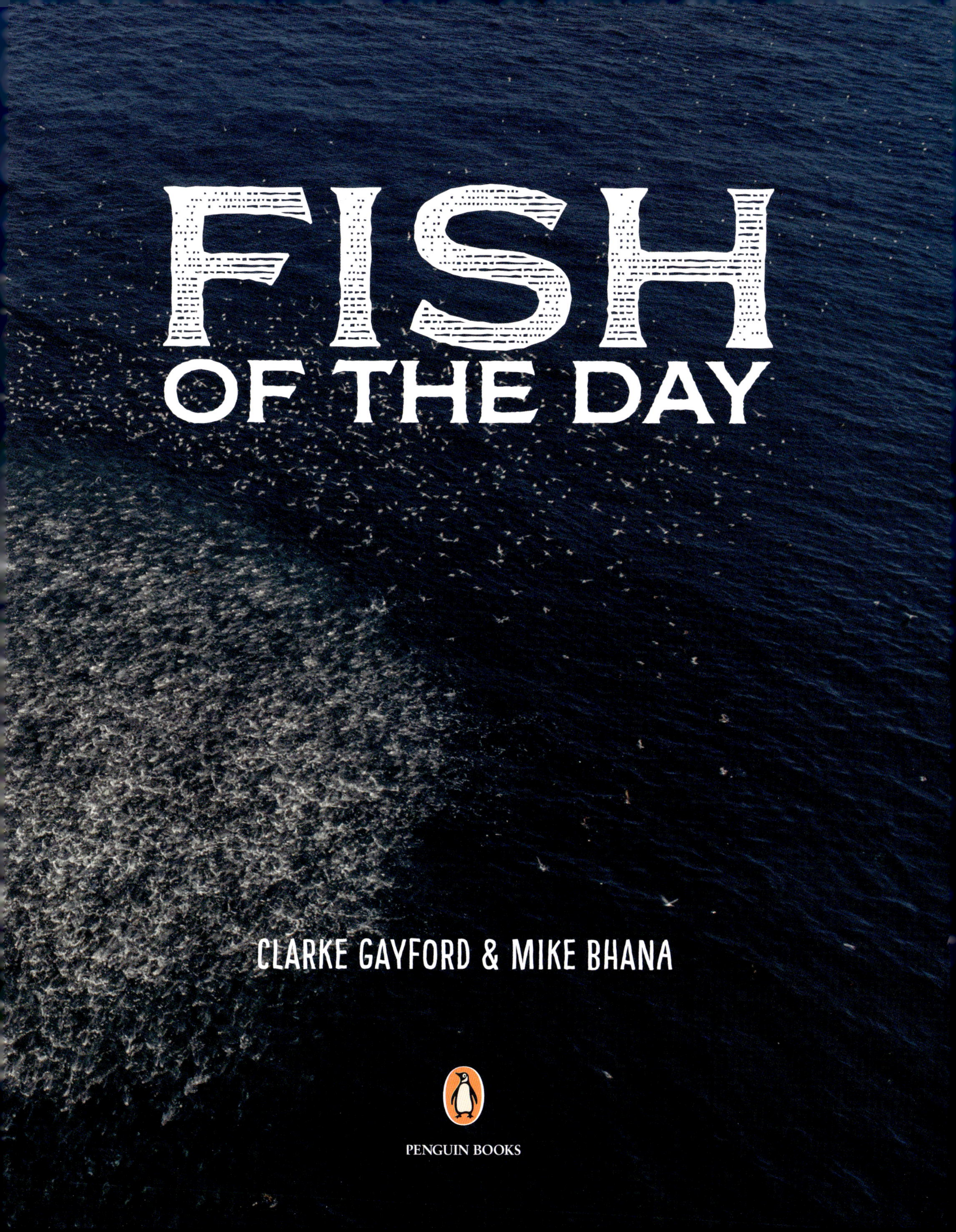

FISH
OF THE DAY

CLARKE GAYFORD & MIKE BHANA

PENGUIN BOOKS

PENGUIN

UK | USA | Canada | Ireland | Australia
India | New Zealand | South Africa | China

Penguin is an imprint of the Penguin Random House group of companies, whose addresses can be found at global.penguinrandomhouse.com.

Penguin
Random House
New Zealand

First published by Penguin Random House New Zealand, 2021

10 9 8 7 6 5 4 3 2

Cover design by Carla Sy © Penguin Random House New Zealand
Text design by Carla Sy and Katrina Duncan © Penguin Random House New Zealand
Cover photograph by Mike Bhana
Illustrations by Cameron Orr
Front cover: Clarke with a feisty giant trevally caught in Samoa.
Back cover: The mahimahi of a lifetime off the coast of Niue.
Prepress by Image Centre Group
Printed and bound in China by 1010 Printing

A catalogue record for this book is available from the National Library of New Zealand.

ISBN 978-0-14-377623-9

penguin.co.nz

MIX
Paper from responsible sources
FSC® C016973

For Neve Te Aroha and her patient mum.
— CLARKE GAYFORD

To my beautiful wife, my four wonderful children,
my sister and Dad and late Mum who have all
supported me on my life journey exploring
and filming the Pacific and beyond. Thanks for
the understanding and encouragement
when so many questioned.
— MIKE BHANA

CONTENTS

INTRODUCTION

In 1986, a skinny little 10-year-old kid from rural Gisborne already knew what he wanted to do when he grew up. It was hardly surprising, considering his dad had exposed him to fishing from a very young age. A short story written in Room 3 of Makauri Primary School captured those ambitions: 'I would like to choose for an occupation I would like to be a fisherman . . . I will buy a great big boat. We are going to have a radio in the boat. We are going to have a deepwater sounder.' He was obviously already familiar with the necessary accessories required to become a proper fishing professional. Little did he know then that fishing would eventually find him later in life wrapped up in a TV show. As I'm sure you've worked out by now, that young guy was me.

My entire childhood revolved around the sea. My early years on the water were split between Gisborne and the Mahia Peninsula, on the North Island's east coast, fishing, diving and surfing. Living there, it's impossible for the ocean not to have an influence on your life. Such was my obsession with fishing that I even committed to learning all the Latin and Māori names of the local fish at a young age.

But when I left home, I also left the sea. I headed off in other directions but always felt like something was missing.

Many years later, I had become increasingly disheartened with the work I was doing. I felt as if the radio station I had been working for had lost its

Pages 2–3
Casting to a cloud of surface-feeding trevally and kahawai off the Mokohinau Islands in the Hauraki Gulf.

Pages 4–5
Fly fishing with Louie the Fish at one of Louie's secret trout lakes in his 'classic' Kiwi tinnie in the central North Island.

Opposite page
A lucky lifetime of mucking about on the sea.

creative flair, and I was feeling too old and tired to keep DJing clubs and festivals.

I remember seeing an interview with fisheries research scientist Dr Catherine Chambers about the connection fishermen have to the sea and to their communities, in which she said: 'Fishing is not a job, it's a livelihood and it is bound by place. When those things separate from each other, all of the social aspects start to break down. You get into real problems with isolation, depression, anxiety, nervousness about the future. All of these are very personal, but they're also very real impacts that affect the psychological and even physical wellbeing in people.' I certainly missed my connection to Gisborne, but more than that, I missed my connection to the ocean.

Then, as luck would have it, I had the opportunity to buy a small boat, which gave me back that taste of the sea. There is something deeply rewarding about heading off out into the blue and returning with food, line-caught or speared. I realised that it was this connection, this sense of fulfilment that I had been missing all these years.

I consciously decided that I wanted that back in my life, so I needed to find a way to make a job of it. Realising this connection was also the perfect excuse to relive what I had lost when I left Gisborne — and to go and have a series of adventures of a lifetime.

When my long-time friend and film industry legend Mike Bhana returned to live full time in New Zealand after 25 years of documentary making in the Pacific, we decided to take a chance on a format created over a few beers. My thinking was 'Well, if it all fails, at least I will have spent a year fishing and diving around the Pacific, having experiences money can't buy.' By treating it like the OE I never really had, I figured I couldn't really lose.

Thankfully the momentum of *Fish of the Day* kept going, and six years later I am writing this book, stuffed full of moments I will forever cherish. In this time I've been lucky enough to explore all corners of New Zealand, but much further afield as well. Through making the show I have learned so much more about our oceans and the people connected to them than I ever thought possible.

On an early trip to Rarotonga, someone described the Pacific to me as 'The Blue Continent', and that expression has resonated ever since. On a world map, the Pacific Ocean appears as a big blue expanse, but zoom in and you discover that, far from being empty, it is peppered with islands.

Spending time in countries such as Fiji, Samoa, Rarotonga, Niue, Tahiti, Hawaii, Vanuatu and the Solomons, among others, I began to appreciate not just the scale of diversity between these places, but within them too. The Solomon Islands are a great example. The name is a clumsy title for a disparate group of hundreds of islands spread over 24,000 sq km, where around 70 different languages are spoken. It's peopled by a rich blend of Melanesians who are not only physically different between areas, but who have starkly differing cultures and traditions. For example, on one island a boy's rite of passage to manhood is determined by the solo capturing of a fearsome deep-sea fish we know as the Peruvian oilfish. The boy must then eat the entire fish himself, as the village watches on, knowing all too well the powerful laxative effect its flesh has. Their howls of laughter ringing in the boy's ears, he dashes into the bushes, returning a man. Then there are villages where the people fish using spiderwebs, and a small island called Mono where the people celebrate 'New Zealand Day' with song and dance every October 27, commemorating the day in 1943 that Kiwi and American soldiers landed on the island to recapture it from occupying Japanese forces during World War II. And all this just from the Solomon Islands group, a place I've barely scratched the surface of.

Through all the trips we've done, it's the people you meet that leave the most lasting impression — locals and expats alike who have forged a livelihood out of their own little pocket of paradise, from charter boat captains and tropical resort owners, to local guides and creators of tourist attractions built around the natural assets of the area. A consistent theme runs through the stories of the fantastic operators we have been lucky enough to work with: that of choosing a lifestyle over riches, of doing whatever they can to stay close to something they love and have a deep passion for. This has made it incredibly difficult for us here at *Fish of the Day* to watch them from a distance being so adversely affected by the ravages of Covid-19. Holed up and hanging on, some are barely able to make ends meet as they sit out a pandemic, cut off from their tourist lifeblood. I, for one, am looking forward to the day when we can meet up with old friends again and forge new relationships.

The other thing you consistently learn on all these trips is just how much you do not know. This is never more evident than when it comes

to fishing. Fishing truly is the most addictive real-life puzzle you could ever hope to be obsessed with. It's a constant state of problem-solving, with more variables than a thousand-square chessboard. Even having the grandest of acquired fishing 'knowledge' will only get you to a place where it's possible to glimpse into the void of just how much you do not know. Be it for recreational, commercial or customary purposes, the condition of 'fishing' doesn't just get under your skin, it *becomes* your skin. It's a life pursuit that pursues you for a wholeness of life, if you should be so lucky.

Today, the highest compliment I am paid echoes along the lines of 'I love your fishing show, and I don't even like fishing'. In that statement exists a small tell of our secret agenda on *Fish of the Day*: subtly introducing new people to the oceans that surround them. It is a concept we have nurtured from the beginning. We believe that if you can give people a personal connection to something, they are much more likely to start caring about it. We wanted to create a show that viewers enjoyed, but that would also send them away thinking the odd question about where the fish they eat comes from. Was it sustainably caught? How do I feel about crashing fish stocks, increased pollution, unbalanced ecosystems and our management of it all? It is our mission to weave these considerations into a TV show where we use fishing as the excuse to show off incredible travel destinations.

We call this spinning ball of blue mass we live on Earth, which goes some way to demonstrating how we have long dismissed its true colour. Like us, the bulk of this planet is made up of water. It is easy to forget what is often out of sight, but we hope that our deep personal connection to the sea and our environmental messages have brought you a little closer to our watery but incredibly fragile backyard.

Opposite page
The mahimahi of a lifetime off the coast of Niue.

Clarke Gayford
Auckland, 2021

1

MOUNTAINS TO THE SEA

LOCATION
WANAKA, NEW ZEALAND

FISH OF THE DAY
BROWN TROUT

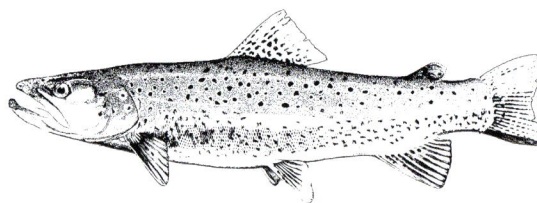

Central Otago has a true continental climate: hot, dry summers that contrast with cold, crisp winters. It is an alpine playground, with white, snow-capped mountains feeding luminous green rivers that flow through alpine valleys into deep blue lakes. But of all the rich colours that this place displays, there's one in particular that many people travel here to see: brown.

Brown is not normally a colour you would associate with speed, cleverness and agility, but those are all the traits of the brown trout. It is a fish that has adapted so well to New Zealand, its adopted country, that the largest ever taken on a rod and reel anywhere in the world was caught just up the road from Wanaka. I didn't go there in hopes of a world record, but right from the start of my *Fish of the Day* journey, there have been a couple of things I really wanted to achieve. The first was to catch a dogtooth tuna both on rod and reel and with a spear (see chapter 8 for that story), and the other was to join the double-figure club by catching a trout weighing over 10 pounds (4.5 kg). I knew that any fish that big would be released, so on this trip I also wanted to catch a couple of smaller ones as well, for the pan.

Previous spread
Minaret Station sits at 1000 m in a picturesque glacial valley in the Southern Alps.

Wanaka today is basically a resort town — a gateway to the Southern Alps and Mount Aspiring National Park, true *Lord of the Rings* country. It's hard to believe that what's on offer here is shared by a resident population of just 9000. But this is no ordinary town, nor has it always been about tourism. With its richer older sibling Queenstown just over the ranges to the south, Wanaka has grown up exactly as you'd expect of a younger child left to its own devices.

And by rich I mean gold, which was where it all started in terms of European settlement. Being so far from the coast and access to provisions, the people who settled here back in the 1860s, gold pans in hand, had to be resourceful, resilient and creative. It is why this town and its people are so grounded today. In those days, if you couldn't fix it, design it or build it yourself, you didn't survive. That make-or-break attitude is still evident even today, as people channel their creativity, energy and passion for the outdoors into new ways of making a living.

Wanaka and the mountains and alpine meadows it sits amongst are a true adventurers' paradise. There's great skiing, mountain climbing, mountain biking, fishing, kayaking, jet boating, hunting and hiking. But for me, Wanaka was all about the fish. Whether you're a purist with the fly or a 'cast-a-spinner' kind of fisherman, there are plenty of opportunities here, in both river and lake. Every body of water is alive with both brown and rainbow trout, and there are plenty of great guides who'll get you on the fish, too.

I was lucky enough to hook up with a chap by the name of Gordy Watson. One of his best lines (and by no means his only one) was this pearler: 'It's not all lollipops and ice creams out here every day, mate, but it's a pretty nice place to be.' I loved his humour and can thoroughly recommend him as a guide, especially if that artful dance of casting, timing and skilfully serving hand-tied make-believe fish snacks to unsuspecting monster river trout is your thing.

We choppered in to fish the Hope River, on the western side of the Main Divide in the Mount Aspiring National Park. This river was so remote

that the fish had very little experience of anglers, hopefully making my job of hooking one just that much easier. Fly fishing has never really been my strong point, but thanks to Gordy's skills and knowledge, after a few hours of perseverance I was hooked up to a solid brown.

Brown is not normally a colour you would associate with speed, cleverness and agility, but those are all the traits of the brown trout.

It was a really good fish, pulling line and running up and down the river as we stumbled our way along the bank, trying to keep it out of the logs and big boulders. When it finally broke the surface it looked like a 10-pounder for sure. Then off it ran again. On every run, my heart was in my mouth, hoping that tiny hook wouldn't pull out.

Another 10 minutes later we finally had it in range. With one swoop of his net, Gordy had our fish. The result was my best result in a South Island river to date but not quite an invitation to join that exclusive double-figure club.

The following morning, I had just enough time for another great wee adventure — a paddle on the lake itself with Paddle Wanaka. Chris and Bex Thornton, who set up the business, are a typical Wanaka couple, their lives revolving around this incredible outdoor playground. Chris took me for a paddle to Ruby Island — a little island with a big history.

There used to be a tearoom and Saturday-night cabaret out there in the late 1920s. Locals would head out in boats for parties which were officially 'dry', but plenty of alcohol was smuggled in. Sitting on the shores of the island you can imagine the scenes from those days.

There was one other place I'd heard stories about that I was keen to visit: Minaret Station, an isolated lodge set 1000 m above sea level in a hidden mountain valley. The only way to get there is by helicopter, or by boat followed by a long walk or mountain-bike ride. It's a gateway to

Opposite above
The iconic Ruby Island in Lake Wanaka is a great day trip by kayak or boat.

Opposite below
With guide Chris Thornton from Paddle Wanaka on our way to Ruby Island.

Following spread
The view from our helicopter as we head out over Lake Wanaka towards Minaret Station.

'I grew up around here. I kind of just used to be tacked on to the side of my grandad walking around. He used to tell all his mates I was teethed on a fly rod, so I got off to a pretty good start.'

— GORDY WATSON, TROUT GUIDE

activities like heliskiing, trekking, mountain biking, hunting and fishing and is part of the Alpine Group, set up way back in the 1960s by legendary aviator Sir Tim Wallis, AKA Hurricane Tim.

He's a bit of a legend in these parts. Actually, that's an understatement. Sir Tim purchased his first helicopter way back in 1965, so, more than a decade before I was even born, he was tearing up the skies and writing New Zealand's early helicopter history. He was one of the pioneers of live deer-recovery back in the 1970s. Gunners would literally hang off the skids of the helicopters shooting nets at running deer while pilots like Sir Tim skilfully weaved their way through the rugged alpine wilderness.

But it didn't end there. Sir Tim went on to restore an entire collection of World War II fighter planes and set up the hugely successful Warbirds over Wanaka event.

He's not come out of it unscathed, though. A helicopter crash in 1968 left him partly paralysed in his left leg, and a Spitfire crash or two in the '80s and '90s also took their toll.

Sir Tim's legacy as a pioneer of deer farming in New Zealand and an avid supporter of multiple charities, as well as his current business operations including Alpine Helicopters and Minaret Station, make him one of the biggest contributors to Wanaka's economy.

Minaret is a working high-country station of over 20,000 ha, home to around 10,000 deer, 7000 sheep and over 1000 head of cattle. The lodge was built to give international guests a luxurious taste of New Zealand's spectacular back country. I managed to hitch a lift up with Alpine Helicopters, attempting to grab a couple of trout for lunch on the way.

We set the chopper down in an isolated bay on the edge of the lake. Close by, two small streams emptied slightly murky stains into the blue of the bay.

As soon as we walked up to the first one, we spotted a nice brown sitting on the edge of the bank. A few casts of a soft bait and I was in — not

a big brown but perfect for lunch. In the next stream was another. Here the water was so shallow the trout's fins were out of the water, making it extremely difficult to cast to. But as soon as I got my little paddle-tail soft bait in view it pounced, and a short fight later I had lunch all wrapped up. I don't think I've ever had freshwater fishing so easy!

We planned to stay the night up at Minaret, and Alastair Wilson, the head chef, suggested we add a wee dog-leg to our journey to grab a little surf to go with our venison. This meant heading around 70 km to the west as the crow or, in my case, the Squirrel flies, to get some pāua. Getting to this wild and isolated stretch of the South Island's west coast required us to cross New Zealand's Southern Alps. Here's the tricky bit: it was cloudy and, as helicopters cannot fly through cloud, we needed to either stay under it, go around it or go over it. Going 3500 m up was the chosen route. All this for a few pāua! But what a ride — the scenery breathtaking at every valley, clifftop, tarn and hidden river we crossed.

Once over the Main Divide, we tracked down from the mountains to the coast on the edge of Fiordland National Park. This is as isolated as you can get — it would take weeks to walk into the spot we landed at — but we didn't have to go much further to find our pāua. There were literally hundreds at my feet in less than a metre of water. Everywhere I looked, there were big fat pāua stuck to the rocks. Too easy! Then we had another stunning flight back to the lodge to spend the afternoon mountain biking and hiking before Al cooked up a sumptuous meal.

Wanaka — what a spot and what a great bunch of locals.

HOT SMOKED BROWN TROUT

ALASTAIR WILSON — MINARET STATION
SERVES 2

1 brown trout
½ teaspoon fennel powder
½ teaspoon coriander seeds
½ teaspoon cumin
pinch salt
½ teaspoon black pepper
½ cup brown sugar
bourbon or rum
mānuka chips

Salad
equal quantities of radicchio
   (could use red cabbage as a
   substitute), shaved fennel and
   sliced courgette (a handful of
   each will make plenty of salad
   for two)
12 grapes, quartered, pips
   removed
2 tablespoons slivered almonds
½ Granny Smith apple,
   julienned or cut into
   matchsticks
2 tablespoons quality olive oil
a good squeeze of lemon juice

Sauce
100 g crème fraîche
2 tablespoons chopped chives
seasoning to taste

Take the fillets off the trout (skin on) and pin bone them.

Mix the fennel, coriander seeds, cumin, salt and black pepper with
the brown sugar, add bourbon to form a sticky paste and apply
to the flesh side of the fish. This can be done the night before,
allowing the fish to marinate overnight in the fridge for maximum
taste.

Soak the mānuka chips in a 4:1 mixture of water and bourbon for at
least an hour. Dry off the chips (use a sieve) and add to the bottom
of your smoker.

Put the smoker on the heat and wait till the chips start to smoke,
not steam. You will smell this start to happen.

Add the fish to the smoker and cover for seven to eight minutes or
longer for larger fish.

Combine the salad ingredients with a generous amount of quality
olive oil and a squeeze of lemon juice.

Combine sauce ingredients.

Plating instructions
Put a couple of tablespoons of the sauce onto the plate, break the
smoked trout into large pieces and scatter over the plate. Top with
salad and serve.

2

IN THE FOOTSTEPS OF JFK

LOCATION
SOLOMON ISLANDS

✕

FISH OF THE DAY
GREEN JOBFISH

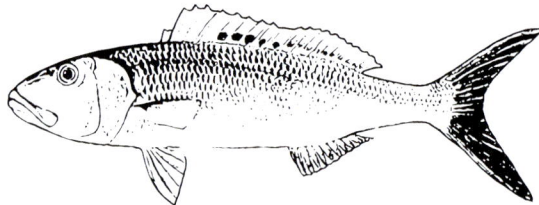

It looks like one of the most untouched and forgotten places on Earth, but it has not always been this idyllic. During World War II the Solomon Islands archipelago became the site of some of the bloodiest and most brutal battles in the Pacific.

Today its sandy shores and crystal-clear tropical waters are littered with the remnants of conflict. The wrecks and debris form vast underwater ecosystems, where great clouds of fish swim, creating an angler's El Dorado like no other.

One of the great thrills of a journey is the anticipation — not knowing what you're going to see, or what to expect. That was what I felt before I travelled to the Solomon Islands to chase an unusual species called the green jobfish. They can be hard to catch on a rod and exceptionally tricky to spear, but they also happen to be one of the tastiest fish in the sea.

But it wasn't the anticipation of chasing the jobfish, or even fishing at all, that first sparked my interest in the Solomons. It was retracing the steps of another journey — the one John F Kennedy took aboard his torpedo patrol boat, PT 109, during World War II — that I was most excited about. Kennedy came to these waters in 1943 as part of his US naval service in the Pacific, a journey that took him halfway around the world, to fight his way through over 900 islands inhabited by just half a million people, speaking around 70 different languages; a journey that ended with the sinking of his boat and very nearly the loss of a future president of the United States of America.

The Solomons was the site of one of the most brutal campaigns in the Pacific during World War II. More than 10,000 Allied soldiers were killed here, as well as a staggering 86,000 Japanese, but it wasn't just the military from both sides of the conflict that suffered loss of life — thousands of locals, too, were lost. This battlefield took an enormous toll on the Solomon Islanders, a people caught up in a foreign war on their own soil.

One of the many stories of wartime bravery relates to the locals who saved JFK's life. After PT 109 was sunk by a Japanese destroyer, JFK and 10 of his crew made it to a small island but needed to send a message to let his superiors know they had survived. It was a local Solomon Islander who risked his life to do it; JFK carved a message on a coconut and islander Eroni Kumana paddled a canoe through Japanese-held territory to deliver the news. The coconut was returned to JFK and years later, when he became US president, he put it on his desk in the White House to remind himself of the selfless attitude and generosity of the local Solomon Islanders who saved his life.

To find the elusive green jobfish, I teamed up with the fishing guides from Zipolo Habu Resort on Lola Island. Jobfish can get to a decent size — the world record is just over 20 kg or 44 pounds — and to target this fish we headed to the edge of the reef to cast poppers.

Casting poppers along an almost untouched reef edge is an absolute adrenaline rush. You simply don't know what is going to roar up from the reef below and devour your lure. And that is the other thing about popper or stick-bait fishing: because the lure is floating on the surface, you get to see the strike as the fish, head out of the water, attempts to swallow it.

We had a fish take almost every cast, including a blacktip reef shark that hit like a freight train. Who knew they could move so fast! Then, after a dozen or more fish, came a swirl and a take. Suddenly I was in a real fight. I didn't get a clear ID on the fish when it struck, but I knew I needed to get it away from the reef before it dived back into the coral hole it came from.

Whatever was on the end of my line had some serious attitude, forcing me to risk putting more drag on to keep it out of the razor-sharp coral. Back and forth it ran along the reef edge, as I shouted for the boat driver to head out into deeper water. It simply didn't give in, and this for me was the first hint that it might just be my target. Green jobfish are revered for their fight, so you could imagine my relief when I finally caught a glimpse of it as it came to the boat. It was solid too, around 4 kg. I love it when a plan comes together!

Green jobfish are revered for their fight, so you could imagine my relief when I finally caught a glimpse of it as it came to the boat. I love it when a plan comes together!

With the green jobfish on ice, we headed north by boat towards Blackett Strait, where JFK's patrol boat was sunk. Along the way we were lucky enough to be shown a piece of history that pre-dated JFK's wartime adventures, at one of the most eerie places I have ever set foot in.

The people of the island of Gizo were once notorious headhunters, who decapitated their enemies, and where did they store the captured heads? On Skull Island, of course. Seeing the skulls up close you quickly realise that these are not cheap souvenirs that you buy in a novelty store — they all once belonged to people, conquests of the Gizo tribe.

No trip to the Solomons would be complete without a few wreck-dives, starting with some of the planes and ships up around Munda in the western Solomons. You can see wrecks such as Jim Dougherty's Dauntless dive bomber, sitting almost untouched on the bottom of the ocean after crash-landing on July 23, 1943. Jim and his gunner both managed to

Opposite above
The anticipation of a new destination. The longboat ride from Gizo to Imagination Island, Solomons.

Opposite below
The islands that John F Kennedy and PT 109 used as a base during World War II, just a few kilometres from Munda in the Solomon Islands.

escape with their lives; in fact, Jim returned 52 years later, to the exact minute, to be photographed climbing back into the cockpit.

Also in Munda is the Peter Joseph WWII Museum, set up and run by local Solomon Islander Barney Paulsen. After finding the dog tags of a US serviceman, Peter Joseph Palatini, in 2002, Barney has been collecting war relics ever since.

Tracking down those tags started an obsession. He bought a metal detector and, well, the rest is history — World War II history. Everything in the museum Barney has recovered from around his house and the hills behind. There are hundreds of dog tags like Peter Palatini's on display, both American and Japanese, along with all sorts of incredible pieces of this area's history, including boxes of old grenades. Barney certainly has some pretty funny gardening stories: 'Well, sometimes when harvest comes, we are unaware they're there, together with the potatoes. Potato, potato, potato — oops, grenade. Exciting gardening.'

Further south around Guadalcanal there are a couple of must-see, must-dives, particularly for New Zealanders. I wanted to visit one wreck in particular, to pay my respects to HMNZS *Moa*, the only New Zealand naval vessel lost to enemy fire during World War II.

She sits in around 45–50 m of water, so it's a deep dive. It's dark and eerie down there, with a squadron of giant batfish guarding what is still today a war grave. She was hit by a 500-pound bomb during a raid by the Japanese on April 7, 1943, going down in just three and a half minutes. Five New Zealanders went down with her.

The boat is easily recognisable as the minesweeper she was, with the depth-charge racks sitting on deck, still with a few charges in place. As I swam along her 50 m length I felt a real sense of loss for those families whose fathers, sons, brothers and uncles still lay entombed in her hull.

The Solomon Islands was surely worthy of my anticipation. It's an extraordinary destination, the people are amazing and the fishing and diving are exceptional.

'Well, sometimes when harvest comes, we are unaware they're there, together with the potatoes. Potato, potato, potato — oops, grenade. Exciting gardening.'

— BARNEY PAULSEN, SOLOMON ISLANDS

CEVICHE SOLOMONS STYLE

MUNDA VILLAGE
SERVES 2

fresh, white-fleshed fish
several limes (we used
  bush limes)
1 fresh coconut
1 tomato
1 capsicum
2 onions
fresh chilli to taste
salt

Fillet the fish, removing all bones, and cut into small, bite-sized cubes. Put these cubes into a bowl and squeeze lime juice over the top, until the fish is soaked.

Let the fish 'cook' in the lime juice for 2–5 minutes — you'll notice the juice making the edge of the fish cubes become opaque. Drain off any excess lime juice.

Husk and crack a fresh coconut in half, carefully collecting the fresh coconut juice as it pours out. Take each half of the coconut and grind out the flesh inside. Strain the coconut pulp through coconut tree bark, retaining the flesh and pulp for another use if desired. (You probably can also use a thin cloth to strain, but I'm trying to keep the recipe authentic here!)

Cut the tomato into quarters, then remove the pulp and softer centre, leaving only the outer skin and flesh. Cut this skin into small pieces and add to the fish, along with the strained coconut juice. Slice up the capsicum, onion and chilli, and add to the fish for colour and taste.

Add a sprinkle of salt.

Let it stand for a while, then serve. If you have one of those modern refrigerator things, then by all means chill first before serving.

SOLOMONS FISH CURRY

SERVES 2

cooking oil
1 onion, chopped
2 tablespoons finely diced
  fresh ginger
handful chopped cherry
  tomatoes
2 potatoes, chopped into
  2 cm cubes, parboiled
1 tablespoon curry powder
1 teaspoon turmeric
splash of Tabasco sauce,
  to taste
1 trevally, filleted and
  chopped into 2 cm cubes
1–2 cups freshly squeezed
  coconut cream (to cover
  fish)
squeeze of lemon juice

Heat some oil in a wok until the oil is starting to smoke. Add the onion and ginger. Turn down the heat and fry for several minutes until the onion softens.

Add the cherry tomatoes and the parboiled potatoes, and continue to cook. Stir through curry powder, turmeric and Tabasco sauce.

As the vegetables begin to soften, add the fish and stir again. Add the coconut cream and keep stirring through. Turn the heat down low and let it simmer quietly for 10 minutes.

Serve with a squeeze of lemon juice.

3
COROMANDEL CATHEDRALS

LOCATION
EASTERN COROMANDEL PENINSULA, NEW ZEALAND

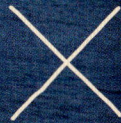

FISH OF THE DAY
BLUENOSE AND PŌRAE

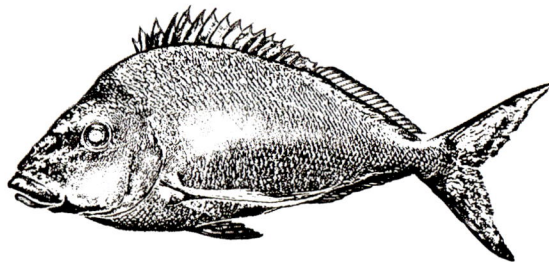

I t was a small town on the east coast of the Coromandel Peninsula where New Zealand's oldest artefact linking us to the sea and our enduring relationship to kaimoana was revealed. Hidden for centuries under an ageing pōhutukawa at the water's edge at Tairua sat what might have seemed to be an insignificant midden. But it proved to be much more important than it initially appeared.

Our coasts are quite literally littered with middens — dump sites for Māori settlements filled not only with discarded shells and other rubbish but with insights into our past. This midden lay untouched for hundreds of years until 1964, when an archaeological dig made an astonishing find: a fishing lure made from the shell of a tropical black-lipped pearl oyster. The midden was dated back to the 1600s or early 1700s and the lure itself, 50 mm long, was revealed by radiocarbon dating to have been made in the early to mid-1300s.

This lure was not only the oldest artefact uncovered in situ on New Zealand soil, but also the only one that can be traced directly back to Polynesia. Lures of this shape and form had been found previously only in archaeological digs on Ua Huka island in the Marquesas, 5500 km to the northeast. It is a direct link between Māori and our Tahitian neighbours, and it offers us a glimpse into the expansiveness of early Polynesian voyaging.

Today that link between people and the sea is still strong in Tairua, which offers great fishing and sublime diving, and has a real sense of community. Local charter-fishing operators such as Carl Muir on *Provider* and Jason Harris on *Strikezone* are as good as it gets, offering a huge range of fishing covering shallow and deep water, as well as game fishing.

I've been lucky enough to fish with both these operators. On one trip aboard *Provider* we headed offshore in search of deep-sea bluenose. I love this type of hunting, as it feels like the final frontier of scaly exploration! We went real deep — as in it taking 17 minutes just to get your bait to the bottom, which represented 360 m down to the tiny seamount we were positioned above. By the end of our session, I worked out that I had hand-wound over 3 km of line.

Here, technology and accuracy are everything when it comes to finding your marks. Get it right and the rewards are enormous: enormous bluenose, enormous ling and enormous bass, which all swim in an environment that has almost no natural light. Some bigger fish took more than half an hour to raise.

With aching arms, legs and shoulders, but plenty of fish, we headed back to Tairua, sending a flurry of text messages to set up another great Coromandel tradition: a locals barbecue. Friends, neighbours and even a couple of freedom campers were invited to share some of the incredible deep-water catch.

Despite our experience, deep-sea fishing is not what *Provider* and its skipper Carl Muir are best known for — it's actually kingfish. A usual day trip out will see many anglers giving up by 10 a.m., their arms too sore to wind any more after catching and releasing fish after fish in the 10–30 kg range. These fish, relative to their weight, are as powerful as they come.

Jason has a great reputation too, targeting the waters around the closer islands for snapper, kingfish and other species, while further offshore he's

got catching the incredible-tasting pink maomao down to an artform.

There is a spectacular amount of coast to explore around here whether you do it with local charter operators, your own boat or on foot. White-sand beaches, rocky headlands and some pretty special cathedrals — of the natural rock kind, that is. The best-known one is Cathedral Cove, north of Tairua, then there is the Blowhole to the east of Hahei — a huge rock chamber with an opening up to the sky — and the second biggest sea cave in the country, near Hot Water Beach.

But it is offshore where you will find one of the most spectacular cathedrals I've ever seen, and it's underwater. Twelve nautical miles out from Tairua are the incredible Alderman Islands. They are a fish magnet of epic proportions, not dissimilar to the Poor Knights Islands except for one major difference: the Aldermans are not in a marine reserve, so you can fish and spearfish here.

I love hunting for deep-sea bluenose, as it feels like the final frontier of scaly exploration.

The diving is something else, and the underwater cathedral on Hongiora Island is an absolute bucket-list adventure. There are three entrances and, when the afternoon light is just right, great shafts of flickering and dancing light rays fill the chambers. If you're brave enough there is also an underwater cave system that takes you right underneath the island.

Diving around these islands you are likely to see huge schools of kingfish, giant packhorse crayfish, and clouds of blue maomao, trevally and a fish I had come to target, pōrae. Pōrae are hard to catch on rod and reel, so for this species I needed my speargun.

I jumped in and was immediately surrounded by bottlenose dolphins. These guys are big, and they come in close. The more you interact, the more they play. After about a half-hour of my swimming around like a mad man entertaining them, they headed off on their hunt while I began mine.

Pōrae love seagrass beds and all the invertebrates that call these underwater pastures home. As soon as I found a good patch of seagrass, I found my pōrae. There were a dozen or so feeding at a depth of around

Opposite above
Hand-feeding kina to red pigfish in the clear waters off the Alderman Islands.

Opposite below
Fishing on *Provider* with Carl Muir and Scott Adamson. Our deep-sea catch: giant bass, ling and bluenose.

'The underwater cathedral on Hongiora Island is an absolute bucket-list adventure. When the afternoon light is just right, great shafts of flickering and dancing light rays fill the chambers.'

— CLARKE GAYFORD

12 m, and spearing a couple for the table took only a few minutes. Then, fish on ice, we headed back to Tairua.

Tairua is not all about fishing, diving and early Polynesian settlers, by the way — on land there is another history that's worth looking into. Behind the town, hidden in the Coromandel Forest Park, is a rich gold and timber history.

Back in 1864 a small sawmill was opened here, and by the 1880s the hills around the town looked like a war zone. Great dams were constructed upriver, and felled trees were dragged or rolled into man-made lakes before the dams were 'tripped', sending a cascade of logs and water crashing down the river. They say that there were times when you could walk from the Tairua settlement to Pāuanui, on the other side of the estuary, across the log jams. Millions of cubic metres of kauri was cut from the peninsula's hills and used locally and offshore.

Then in the 1890s gold was discovered in the hills, and a network of settlements, water races, tram lines and tunnels was built. The area produced over 55,000 ounces of gold, worth more than $137 million at today's prices. Today the tunnels and old shafts are home only to glow worms and native cave wētā.

I look at early photographs of the Coromandel and have mixed emotions, thinking about how it must have looked before European settlers laid siege to the gold seams and kauri stands. I think about the mining's toxic sludge that once sluiced heavy metals down rivers, poisoning estuaries and creating dead zones of ocean all around them. I wonder how clean and clear the coastal waters would have been back before Europeans arrived and felled the trees, opening the hillsides up to erosion. Can you imagine the localised weather patterns generated by the cooling effect of the truly enormous kauri forests? It would have meant almost constant offshore breezes and, as a surfer, that's a tantalising thought.

Today the wounds have almost healed, but the scars remain as a reminder of how long it takes our environment to restore balance.

Previous spread
Hanging motionless in the expanse of 'The Cathedral' — a huge underwater cave system at the Alderman Islands.

Opposite above
Waiting on a seagrass bed at a depth of 12 m for a pōrae to come within range of the spear.

Opposite below
The infamous Tairua one-way bridge, with the Tairua estuary and Pāuanui in the background.

PĀUA RAVIOLI WITH PŌRAE AND RUKAU

NATHANIEL BLOMFIELD
SERVES 4–6

Ravioli dough

large pinch saffron
3 tablespoons hot water
4 eggs, at room
  temperature, lightly
  beaten
pinch salt
2 tablespoons olive oil
500 g strong flour (high
  gluten)

Rukau

1 kg taro leaves (rukau)
2 teaspoons baking soda
1 can coconut cream
1 onion

Pāua filling

2 pāua
2 spring onions
bunch coriander
2 chillies

butter and thyme for
  cooking
1 large pōrae
fresh micro herbs for
  garnish
1 tomato, prepared
  concasse-style (peeled,
  deseeded, finely
  chopped)

Ravioli dough

Place the saffron in the hot water and let it steep for 5 minutes. Combine eggs, salt, olive oil, saffron and water.

Place the flour in a large bowl and form a well in the centre. Pour the egg mixture into the flour well and mix until a stiff dough is formed. Knead by hand for 10 minutes. If the dough is too sticky, sprinkle with additional flour until it comes together.

Cover the dough with plastic wrap or a damp tea towel and let rest for at least 30 minutes.

Rukau

Clean, devein and slice taro leaves. Bring a large pot of water to the boil, and add baking soda.

Add taro leaves to water and simmer for half an hour until the leaves are very, very soft.

In another pot, place the coconut cream and diced onion and simmer until the onion is cooked.

Strain the taro and add to the coconut mixture. Season to taste and bring back to a simmer, until well heated through. You can purée this mixture or eat as is.

Pāua filling

Mince the pāua. Finely chop the other filling ingredients and add to the minced pāua.

Ravioli

Roll out the dough to an even 2 mm thick. Cut into two even sheets. Place blobs of pāua mix (around ¾ teaspoon) on one sheet, appropriately spaced.

Wet the dough around the edges of each pāua blob and add the top layer of dough. Seal the edges of each ravioli by hand and cut between them, making sure each ravioli is sealed.

Cook in boiling water until the ravioli rise to the surface (approximately 5 minutes). Finish by frying gently in a pan with butter and fresh thyme and a tablespoon of the cooking water, to stop the ravioli sticking together.

Pōrae

Scale and fillet the pōrae, leaving the skin on.

Melt butter in a hot pan and cook skin-side down, adding the fresh thyme. When three-quarters cooked, flip to the non-skin side to finish.

To serve

Put one large tablespoon of rukau on each plate. Place three ravioli on top of rukau. Place pōrae, skin-side up, on ravioli. Garnish with fresh herbs and tomato concasse.

ELECTION (OR ANY) NIGHT FISH BITES

CLARKE GAYFORD
SERVES 8, OR SCALE UP TO FEED A CROWD

500 g boneless snapper or any other firm, white-fleshed fish, cut into 2–3 cm strips
½ cup seasoned flour
2 eggs, lightly beaten
1 cup of your crumb of choice (I'm a big fan of freeze-dried panko crumbs, or you can use batter in place of crumbs)
rice bran oil and butter for frying
salt and pepper to taste

To serve
lemon wedges
mayonnaise

Cut fresh fish into generous bite-sized (2–3 cm) pieces, being careful to remove all bones.

Dust the fish pieces in flour, shaking off any excess. Dip into egg and coat in crumbs. Finish crumbing all fish before cooking.

Put a generous covering of rice bran oil and a small dollop of butter in a deep, wide fry pan and wait until the butter is frothing.

Fry fish in batches for a short time (1–2 minutes) on each side. Drain well on paper towels before plating, to drain any excess oil.

This serves up perfectly as finger food on a large plate with mayonnaise and lemon wedges.

A few tips

- This is an easy way to serve fish to big groups that also helps it go further, giving everyone a chance to try your catch, no matter how small! It can't be used to hide old fish, but does effectively give plain fish a bit of extra flavour.

- Get fish to room temperature before cooking. This will ensure it cooks through more evenly without leaving a raw middle.

- Be generous with the oil. When cooking crumbed fish, I always prefer rice bran oil over olive oil for the higher flash point.

- Put thicker pieces in first, followed by smaller bits towards the end, so they complete the cooking process together.

- While simple, there's plenty of creativity to be had in this space and I've seen a surprising variety of ingredients tried successfully. From a dash of curry powder mixed through flour to a coating of Cajun spice, a bag of crushed salt and vinegar crisps or corn chips, to a slug of beer mixed with pepper and flour. Take your pick!

4

MARLIN MAGIC

LOCATION
TUTUKAKA AND
THE POOR KNIGHTS ISLANDS,
NORTHLAND, NEW ZEALAND

✕

FISH OF THE DAY
MARLIN AND HĀPUKU

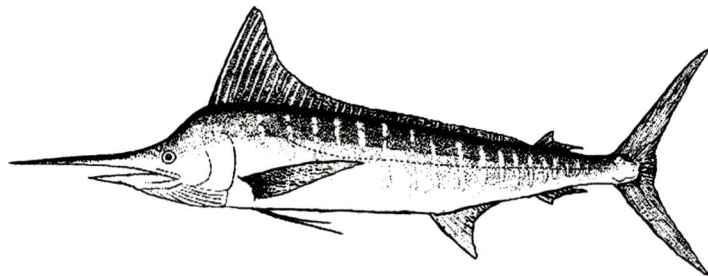

No one really knows why the Poor Knights were called that by Captain James Cook, splashing names about as he carried out his coastline cartography. The Māori name for the group is Tawhiti Rahi, and they're a scraggly collection of weather-gnarled pillars, remnants of a 10-million-year-old volcanic cone standing 23 km off the Tutukaka Coast.

This marine sanctuary was considered by famed French underwater explorer Jacques Cousteau as one of his top-10 dive sites in the world — although if you'd asked our own famed marine biologist Wade Doak, who was out studying the islands when Jacques came to visit, 'It was a shame he didn't come on a good day — he may have ranked it higher.' Having spent more time out there than most, Wade understood just how good this place can get.

It's hard to know where to begin explaining the diversity of life found here, both above and below the water. The rock structure alone is a geologist's dream, with sea tunnels so large on several islands that you can drive a boat right through them. It's also home to the world's largest sea

Previous spread
Glenn McFarlane watches on as I prepare to dive Northern Arch at the Poor Knights Islands.

cave by volume, able to accommodate three large dive-boats at once.

Dive below the surface, however, and a lifetime of discoveries exists in just the sea sponges, soft corals and vibrant collection of marine plants that cling to the rock walls. Then there is the fish life. The islands are far enough offshore to be brushed by an eastern current not present on the coast, which brings in many species not seen closer to the mainland, including warmer-water visitors. In the summer months, the tropical blue water also comes in, providing up to 30 m of visibility.

Dive below the surface and a lifetime of discoveries exist in just the sea sponges, soft corals and vibrant collection of marine plants that cling to the rock walls.

But, as good as it is, it used to be so much better. All too often we are lulled into a false sense of having done the right thing by creating our marine reserves, but they represent just a fraction of our marine space, and unfortunately most fish don't recognise boundaries. This means that many transiting species have disappeared, as fish stocks fall along this part of the coast. So while the Knights still swarm with clouds of resident fish, including pink and blue maomao, kahawai and reef fish like the charismatic Sandager's wrasse, almost all other species have dramatically declined.

Wade Doak QSM — writer, conservationist, diver, photographer and filmmaker — died in 2019, along with another of New Zealand's best-known champions of the marine space, Dr Roger Grace. These two led this country in the areas of marine conservation and ecology. I was lucky enough to sit down with Wade before he died and talk about his history with the Poor Knights Islands, an interview I will never forget.

Wade was one of my heroes, and was instrumental in the establishment of the Poor Knights Islands Marine Reserve. He lamented the loss of the huge schools of hāpuku he once swam with at the Knights in shallow waters. Nearly completely gone, too, are spiny red rock lobster and packhorse crayfish; having been fished almost to collapse outside the reserve, they have all but disappeared from within.

'We look on all fish as fish. But actually they've all got different life histories. They've all got different fecundities. They're millions of years old and they've never had a predator like us,' Wade said. 'So I think that as predators we've got a responsibility to maintain our food security, not destroy it. We've called ourselves sapiens — wise. Let's live up to it and learn to understand what each fish's lifestyle is and how much we can exploit it, or whether we can exploit it at all.'

Wade inspired a generation to seek change, and I would love nothing more than to help realise his dream of restored abundance. Our conversation reminded me of how short our memories are, and how 'shifting baselines' often mask the huge declines in almost all of our coastal fish species.

World-renowned fisheries expert and marine biologist Dr Daniel Pauly coined the phrase 'shifting baselines' back in 1995. 'Every person will have a beginning point relating to their impression of the natural world around them — a benchmark or baseline for assessing changes that they will have. They will notice in the course of their life the changes that they have seen. But what their parents or grandparents had experienced is not in the same category and it is not added to the loss that they have experienced.' It's an important concept to remember as we manage fisheries going forward.

There was a lot of resistance when the marine reserve at the Poor Knights was first proposed in the 1970s, but as is so often the case, when locals began to see the benefits, perspectives soon changed. Some of the early detractors are now fierce protectors of its restrictions.

Today operators such as Dive Tutukaka run multiple island trips daily. Pre-Covid, the throng of tourists — around 14,000 per annum, over half of which were international — was bringing an estimated $10 million of economic activity into the area each year. It's an economic lifeline, with the reserve contributing a staggering $200 million directly to the local economy

Opposite above
Heading towards the famous Blue Maomao Arch at the Poor Knights Islands.

Opposite below
One of my heroes, the late Wade Doak — legend in the marine conservation world.

'As predators, we've got a responsibility to maintain our food security, not destroy it. Let's learn to understand what each fish's lifestyle is and how much we can exploit it, or whether we can exploit it at all.'

— DIVE LEGEND WADE DOAK, 1940–2019

> **The big question with a marlin is always: is it actually hooked, or are the hooks just hanging onto the bill?**

since its inception 40 years ago — and all of this because people like Wade Doak had the gumption and energy to push hard for a reserve at a time when people had little concept of what it could offer in return. Now it sits as a tangible glimpse of what an abundant fishery could look like.

You don't need to be a diver to enjoy an incredible day out at the islands — you don't even have to snorkel or to leave the boat to thoroughly enjoy a trip. And while you can't fish at the Poor Knights, further out to sea the rich, warm, tropical waters of summer are a haven for game species such as tuna and marlin.

It was out here, after a thoroughly enjoyable few days of diving, that I went looking for my fish of the day. I had caught blue marlin in the tropics, but never managed to hook a striped marlin. So, with local fishing guru Glenn McFarlane at the helm, out to sea we went.

Glenn's caught over 200 marlin in the 30 years he's been fishing — in fact, I'm pretty sure he can smell them, because within seconds of him saying 'Water's looking good through here, mate', we were hooked up to my very first stripey. And boy do these guys fight hard! In just a few seconds, a couple of hundred metres of line was gone from my reel. Then the win some, lose some game began.

The big question with a marlin is always: is it actually hooked, or are the hooks just hanging onto the bill? Every time the fish changes course, there is a real chance you could lose it, and this is where Glenn's skill came in — keeping the fish travelling in the same direction. Every jump, every run, my heart was in my mouth.

We went from almost to the leader back to half a spool of line half a dozen times. Finally, 40 minutes of serious boat-driving later, Glenn got

Previous spread
Northern Arch. Vibrant sponge-covered walls and the clouds of fish that hang in the current make it one of the best dives in New Zealand.

Opposite above
There are few places on Earth where the colours and variety of sponges, corals and plants are this diverse.

Opposite below
Investigating the detail and variety of life on the rock walls.

hold of the trace and we had our fish to the boat. It was a solid stripey, around the 100 kg mark and in great condition. To say I was ecstatic would be an understatement. True to form, the hooks were literally just tangled around the bill, making for an easy tag and release, and away it swam back into the blue.

Because we'd caught our marlin so quickly, we had time for a quick jig on North Reef to catch something for dinner, but we had to fight the bronze whaler sharks to get a whole kingfish up to the boat. The first couple of hook-ups we simply didn't get control of the fish fast enough, the tell-tale thumps on the line quickly disappearing, replaced by smooth, powerful runs. Sharked!

Two kingie heads later and I pushed my drag to sunset and had another crack. This time I overpowered the hooked kingfish, and with every last ounce of strength I could muster managed to get one to the boat whole. We could see the bronze whalers following it all the way up!

I got out to sea one more time while on the Tutukaka Coast, heading out to find hāpuku, once again with Glenn McFarlane. We arrived at his secret spot late in the day and both Glenn and I sent lines to the bottom, carrying huge sinkers, flashing LED fish-attractors and a couple of circle hooks on a ledger rig with big squid baits. Still hurting from reeling in the marlin a few days earlier, I was hoping we wouldn't have to do too many drops, as hauling the sinkers alone up from 160 m was no easy task.

Luckily, a couple of thumping bites signalled 'fish on', and I started the long retrieve. I know a lot of people use electric reels, but if I'm going to fish, I'm going to do it manually, even if that means paying the price.

Twenty minutes later my line went slack, indicating that the right species was on the end (as hāpuku, bluenose and bass get close to the

> **If I'm going to fish, I'm going to do it manually, even if that means paying the price.**

Opposite page, clockwise from top left
Beyond the Poor Knights the ocean is alive — not just with fish but also with seabirds like this Campbell Island albatross; Two hāpuku from Glenn McFarlane's secret seamount 20 nautical miles offshore; Finally, with the help of legendary skipper Glenn McFarlane, I get my first striped marlin.

Above
Two of Dive Tutukaka's
boats sitting in Nursery
Cove at Poor Knights.

surface, their swim bladders act like lifting bags, and they pop up like balloons). Between us we had three fish in the bin, just like that.

Tutukaka is a great community, full of people all closely connected to the ocean on their doorstep. And where does this sense of community and connection to the environment come from? Well, just over the hill to the south of Tutukaka is Ngunguru. Sitting tucked away here is quite possibly the best little primary school in New Zealand — a school with its own special bell which is rung whenever a pod of dolphins or orca enter the estuary. No matter the lesson, pens are instantly dropped, books slammed shut, and the whole school turns out to excitedly watch and observe the live classroom lesson provided free by nature for all.

As part of their learning curriculum, the kids here have adopted the estuary across the road. Part of this involves monitoring its mauri or life-force. On special field days they race to school, don wetsuits, then off they head over the muddy flats, dodging razor-sharp oyster shells with quick-moving bare feet, before fumbling with flapping flippers to float back on the building flood tide.

Each student is armed with an underwater slate and pen, so they can carefully document the life they see around them. Over time the picture they have been building makes them very aware of any changes. But most importantly they are developing a lifelong connection to the sea.

KINGFISH WITH KAWAKAWA CHIMICHURRI

DEAN THOMPSON, WAHI RESTAURANT, TUTUKAKA
SERVES 4

Kawakawa chimichurri

20 g kawakawa leaves
10 g flat-leaf parsley leaves
10 g coriander leaves
1 shallot
10 g garlic, minced
zest of 2 rocoto chillies
juice and zest of ½ lemon
1 tablespoon pomegranate
   molasses
2 tablespoons moscatel
   vinegar
2 teaspoons caster sugar
2 teaspoons sea salt
cracked pepper
¼ cup extra-virgin olive oil

Croutons

¼ loaf ciabatta, cut roughly
   into cubes
milk, seasoned with salt
   and pepper
4 tablespoons butter

Tomato salad

4 cups roughly sliced
   assorted tomatoes
2 shallots, finely sliced
2 radishes, finely sliced
2 tablespoons roughly
   chopped basil leaves
2 tablespoons roughly
   chopped flat-leaf parsley
   leaves
juice of 1 lemon
sea salt, to taste
cracked pepper, to taste
¼ cup extra-virgin olive oil
100 g goat's cheese

Kingfish

2 tablespoons cooking oil
4 portions kingfish, seasoned
   with salt and pepper
2 tablespoons butter
squeeze of lemon juice
lemon wedges

Kawakawa chimichurri

Finely chop the kawakawa, parsley, coriander and shallot with a sharp knife. Mix with the remaining ingredients. Ideally leave in the fridge for a couple of days before using, to let the kawakawa soften and allow the flavours to come out.

Croutons

Dip the ciabatta into the seasoned milk, then remove and squeeze the excess liquid out of the bread. Sear the croutons in a hot pan with butter to give them colour, then finish them in a 200ºC oven for approximately 5 minutes.

Tomato salad

Gently toss together all the ingredients except the goat's cheese. Add the croutons just before serving.

Kingfish

Heat the oil in a frying pan. Place the fish in the pan and cook till the first side is golden. Flip the fish, then add the butter and a squeeze of lemon. When the fish is just cooked, remove from the pan.

To serve

Place the tomato salad in the centre of the plate, then crumble a little goat's cheese around the edges. Place the cooked fish on top of the salad, and finish with a spoon of the kawakawa chimichurri. Serve with lemon wedges to squeeze.

NAPPE HĀPUKU WITH SWEET CORN, OTAGO COCKLES AND YUZU

RYAN MOORE, THE GROVE
SERVES 6

Hāpuku
4–6 kg hāpuku
rock salt

Yuzu gel
350 ml yuzu juice
150 ml water
10 g agar
40 g sugar

Sweet corn purée
300 g can of sweet corn
  kernels in water
100 ml olive oil
0.5 g xanthan gum
salt to taste
juice of ½ lemon

Pickled enoki mushrooms
200 g enoki mushrooms
oil
flaky sea salt
25 ml chardonnay vinegar

Cockles
1 onion
1 kg Otago cockles
200 ml white wine

Baby corn
4 baby corn
butter
salt

Sweet corn sauce
reserved fish stock (see
  method)
reserved cockle juice (see
  method)
200 ml sweet corn juice
  from can (see method)
300 g butter
salt
lemon juice
borage cress or micro
  herbs for garnish

Hāpuku

Fillet the hāpuku and remove the skin. Make a light stock for the sauce using the bones.

Rub the fish with the salt and let it sit for 8 minutes, then wash off the salt and leave to dry in the fridge for a day, which allows you to get a nice crust on the fish.

Rinse the fish in water to take off the excess salt and cross-cut into 3 cm thick slices. Place the fish in a hot pan with oil. Once cooked halfway through (don't turn the fish) add butter and nappe or spoon the hot foaming butter over the fish as it cooks through. Take off heat and let rest.

Yuzu gel

Place all ingredients into a saucepan and blend with a hand blender until mixed. Bring to the boil, then chill down quickly.

Once the mix has set, place into a blender till smooth.

Sweet corn purée

Place the corn kernels (reserving the liquid for the sweet corn sauce) and olive oil into a blender with xanthan gum and blend until smooth. Season with salt and lemon juice.

Pickled enoki mushrooms

Pick the stalks off the enoki mushrooms. Place a pan on the stove and heat until it's nearly smoking, then add some oil and flash-fry the mushrooms. Add a pinch of flaky salt to bring out the flavour, then deglaze the pan with the vinegar. Continue to cook for a further minute.

Cockles

Place a pan with a lid on the stove and heat until it's really hot. Meanwhile, slice the onion.

Place the cockles and onion into the pan, then add the white wine. Cover with lid and cook for roughly 2 minutes, until all the cockles are open. Take the cockles out of the shells and reserve the juice for the sauce.

Baby corn

Remove the baby corn from their husks and place in a vac pac bag with some butter and salt. If not available, use a ziplock bag with the air removed. Sous vide at 72°C or cook on low in a pot of hot water for 1 hour (note: if fresh baby corn not available, canned baby corn in water will suffice).

When cooked, cut the corn in half lengthwise then brush with oil and finish on the barbecue.

Sweet corn sauce

Take equal quantities of fish stock, cockle juice and corn liquid from the can, and bring to the boil. Dice the butter and drop into the liquid. Wait until it is half melted, then hand-blend until emulsified. Season to taste with salt and a little lemon juice.

Plating instructions

Use wide bowls. Add a solid tablespoon of sweet corn purée. To the side add a mix of the cockles, mushrooms with some cut chives. Opposite side to the sweet corn purée add a half of barbecue baby corn and place the fish on top. On top of the fish add 1 cm drops of the yuzu gel and then finish the dish with some borage cress or micro herbs. Serve with sauce on the side.

5

NORTHLAND ROADIE

LOCATION
NORTHLAND, NEW ZEALAND

FISH OF THE DAY
SNAPPER, SHELLFISH AND SQUID

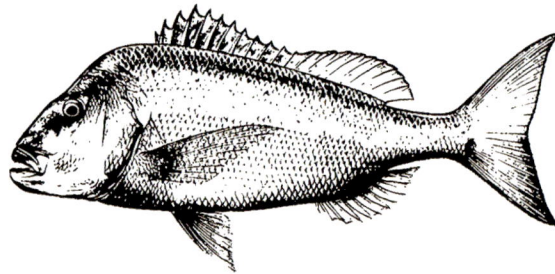

Northland reminds me so much of my hometown of Gisborne that it feels like a home away from home. Deserted white sandy beaches, neglected roads and single-lane bridges; a place in touch with its Māori heritage and the riches of its outdoors, and containing more than a proper pavlova slice of how New Zealand used to be.

It's also a great spot for kaimoana. Where else can you gather cockles, tuatua, mussels, a couple of snapper and a few squid in just a few days?

Many of the first European visitors to the Bay of Islands called the place 'the Hell Hole of the Pacific'. A hundred years later, when famous American western novelist Zane Grey first came to fish there in the 1920s, he dubbed it 'the angler's Eldorado', writing, 'The lure of the sea is some strange magic that makes men love what they fear.' I remember reading these words when I was younger and being intrigued that a place could have such polar-opposite descriptions.

The first stop on my Northland road trip was the Duke of Marlborough hotel in Russell. It's New Zealand's oldest licensed hotel, starting life way

Previous spread
Otehei Bay on Urupukapuka Island in the Bay of Islands, one of Zane Grey's favourite hangouts in the 1920s.

back in 1827, as a place called Johnny Johnston's Grog Shop. Back then, Russell — or Kororāreka, as it was known — was the largest whaling port in the Southern Hemisphere. You can imagine some of the characters who used to roam the streets, causing all sorts of trouble. In December 1835 naturalist Charles Darwin floated in on HMS *Beagle*, anchoring in the bay lined with grog shops and brothels. Needless to say, he didn't find New Zealand at all attractive, writing, 'I am disappointed in New Zealand, both in the country & in its inhabitants' and describing Russell as 'the stronghold of vice'.

I stalled my road trip at Russell to do a bit of a tiki tour around the Bay, joined by a past president of the Bay of Islands Swordfish Club, Bruce Smith. The club is one of the oldest in the country, first incorporated way back in 1918. It was a focus for Zane Grey, and you'll find his name all over the walls: record after record through the 1920s, caught mostly on the *Alma G* — a boat that still plies the waters of the Bay today.

Another club member is Geoff Stone, who ran a boat called *Major Tom* around the Bay for years, catching more than his share of marlin and becoming a bit of a legend for pioneering the art of deep dropping for swordfish. But like many of the fishermen we met on our journeys, Geoff is a conservationist, too, committed to ensuring there are fish in the sea to catch and that we all get to experience the rewards of that, whether it is for the enjoyment of catching or eating.

Snapper was the first species on our list for this trip. The minimum recreational size for snapper is 30 cm from eastern Northland down to the Bay of Plenty, including Auckland, or 27 cm in the rest of the country. They are a fairly accessible species here in the Bay, and it may surprise people to learn the fish's value is significantly greater to the economy if recreationally caught rather than caught and sold commercially.

Let me explain: Kiwis spend over $400 million every year chasing snapper recreationally — that's on trips, equipment, boats, fuel, accommodation, etc. That spend works out to around $88 per kg of snapper caught.

With commercial fishing, 70 per cent of snapper caught are sent overseas, where they are sold whole for around $9 per kg. So that's $9 per kg coming into the New Zealand economy if it's caught commercially, versus $88 dollars if a recreational fisher catches it. This highlights the value of recreationally caught fish and makes a strong argument for protections to ensure there remain good numbers of fish for all fishers.

Zane Grey might have put Russell and the Bay of Islands on the world map because of its incredible fishing, but as with all our fisheries under pressure, restoring abundance is vital to its survival.

A healthy fishery is absolutely essential for places like this 'hell hole'. Zane Grey might have put Russell and the Bay of Islands on the world map because of its incredible fishing, but as with all our fisheries under pressure, restoring abundance is vital to its survival.

Not far out from the Duke, in about 20 m of water, we put down our lines to grab a couple of small snapper or 'pannies'. While I was soft-baiting, my fishing buddy Bruce was sticking to the traditional bait method. We were marking the fish on the sounder and drifting across them. Both bait and plastics were fishing well — in fact, we were one for one on every drift, and within an hour we had enough for a feed.

With fish in the bin it was time to dive the Leander Class frigate HMNZS *Canterbury* — a wreck deliberately sunk for divers out at Deep Water Cove, near the eastern entrance to the bay. At 113 m in length it sits in a calm, sheltered bay, creating a fantastic wreck-dive. It's been on the sea floor since 2007 and is now alive with fish life and covered in kelp and spectacularly coloured sponges — yellows, oranges and reds.

The whole structure is completely encrusted in growth and home to clouds of fish, including snapper, but we are not allowed to fish here, as a voluntary rahui or no-take area has been designated by local Māori, which is keenly observed by everyone.

Heading further north, there's not many areas in this country where you can find yourself swerving on a sandy beach highway to avoid a

Opposite above
Fishing with light tackle increases the experience and becomes a test of skill on big fish.

Opposite below
The reward is being able to hook and land big fish like this 8 kg snapper off the Northland coast.

sunbathing seal that has hauled itself out of the wild surf for a snooze. And just behind that famous Ninety Mile Beach and its flanking dunes, northwest of the Bay of Islands, is a forest alive with herds of wild horses, their noses snorting great clouds of steam as they thunder past my truck.

From driving on seal to driving around seals, the wild, winterless north is a great place to go if you are looking to strip life back to basics. Plenty do, like the seaweed pickers who live in wind-assaulted huts around the rocks from Ahipara, at the southern end of Ninety Mile Beach. No power, no road, no internet, no shops, no bloody worries — a lifestyle increasingly removed from today's hyper-connected existence, yet one far richer in experiences than those of us with a screen stuck in front of our face.

Travel further around these rocks and you'll find magic surf breaks and rocky guts in which to surfcast for your dinner. Here, inshore fish such as kahawai and snapper snuffle along sand edges on incoming tides looking for dislodged crustaceans to complement their diets. Or they might just be looking for shellfish, beds of which are prevalent up and down Ninety Mile Beach. Not just skinny little pipi either, but proper big beds of their larger cousin the tuatua. You can spot them from a distance on a low tide, poking out of the sand. If the reflecting sunlight doesn't give them away, the gathered seagulls certainly do.

Ninety Mile Beach is also home to the protected toheroa, an endangered shellfish that dwarfs even the tuatua in size. Sadly their numbers crashed many years ago due to over-collecting and commercial canning. Despite strict protections there seems to be little sign of improvement in their population, emphasising the dangers of overfishing leading to the collapse of a vulnerable species like this.

The whole tip of the North Island is the proverbial fishermen's basket, such is the abundance and variety of this place. You can spear flounder in the lagoons, catch john dory off the Houhora wharf, gather cockles

Opposite, clockwise from top
4WD beach entry, Te Paki Stream, at the northern end of Ninety Mile Beach on Northland's west coast; Giant kauri Tāne Mahuta in the Waipoua Forest, Northland — this tree is around 2000 years old and 4.4 metres in diameter; With Stu Hofstetter from Paihia Dive and a good snapper taken with a spear in the Bay of Islands.

'The HMNZS *Canterbury* has been on the sea floor since 2007 and is now alive with fish life and covered in kelp and spectacularly coloured sponges — yellows, oranges and reds.'

— CLARKE GAYFORD

Much like coastal Gisborne and Mahia, where I grew up, you can tell this is an area where the sea is still relied upon like a local supermarket.

from the estuaries and even nab yourself a squid in winter around any structure at night with a bit of light. Get yourself a boat, however, and the opportunities blow wide open. From the Three Kings Islands off Cape Reinga for an extreme fishing expedition, to areas like the Garden Patch off Houhora and coastal fishing in the Bay of Islands, the fish are typically all bigger and angrier than anywhere else.

After a couple of days of beach driving and shellfish gathering, we stopped off at a well-known Whangārei Harbour wharf (sorry, can't tell you which one — the locals would kill us) a couple of hours after dark to try to nab a squid. Walking down the wharf, the signs were good: ink splashes everywhere from earlier fishing efforts.

After a couple of casts with my squid jig on the edges of the light pool made by the wharf lights, I got a take. Sure enough it was exactly what we were after, and a good one too. In just a couple of hours we had four nice squid in the bag.

Much like coastal Gisborne and Mahia, where I grew up, you can tell this is an area where the sea is still relied upon like a local supermarket. In the North, outside almost every home you drive past, you can spot boats, small and large, new and old. There are houses surrounded with boxed fishing nets, craypots and buoys; surfcasters on utes; and set-net hook trays, flounder spears and filleting stations made out of old stainless-steel benches out the back or proudly out the front. Here people live closer to the land and sea and all it has to offer, for a simpler way of life. It's my idea of paradise.

Previous spread
Hanging on the anchor chain during my safety stop after diving the HMNZS *Canterbury*.

Opposite, clockwise from top left
Ninety Mile Beach's tuatua beds are among the best in the country and offer great snapper fishing, too; One of the ingredients needed for Luca Villari's Zuppa di pesce alla Siciliana — fresh tuatua; Catching squid on squid jigs off the wharf at night in the Whangārei Harbour.

SNAPPER WITH KAWAKAWA SALSA VERDE, KINA BEURRE BLANC AND URENIKA POTATOES

DAN FRASER, DUKE OF MARLBOROUGH, RUSSELL
SERVES 4

Kawakawa salsa verde

3 cups fresh herbs (I used
   flat-leaf parsley, basil,
   mint, chervil, chives)
1 shallot, peeled
juice of 1 lemon
15 ml red wine vinegar
10 capers
1 gherkin
1 clove garlic
3–4 kawakawa leaves
salt to taste
30 ml light or pure olive oil

Kina beurre blanc

100 ml white wine
100 ml white wine vinegar
1 shallot
5 black peppercorns
2 sprigs thyme
2 bay leaves
50 ml cream
250 g butter, cut into
   small cubes
kina roe from 1 kina
salt and pepper
juice of 1 lemon

Potatoes

20 g butter
100 g smoked bacon,
   cut in strips
1 kg cooked potatoes (I used
   duck-fat confit whole urenika
   potatoes cooked at 150°C for
   45 minutes under fat or oil,
   but you could use boiled or
   roasted)
½ bunch silver beet
salt and pepper

4 fillets snapper, skin on
salt
butter

Kawakawa salsa verde

Blend all ingredients until a smooth paste is achieved, taste and season as required.

Kina beurre blanc

To a pot over a high heat add wine, vinegar, shallot, peppercorns, thyme and bay leaves and reduce until quarter of the original volume (50 ml). Strain the liquid and discard the aromatics.

Reduce the heat to medium and add the cream, then cook down until thick. Turn the heat down to low and slowly whisk in the butter, being careful not to add it too quickly (30–50 g at a time, and allow it to melt before adding more).

Add kina roe to taste, then adjust seasoning and add lemon to your taste.

Potatoes

Add the butter to a medium-hot pan, then bacon, and allow it to crisp a little. Add the potatoes and silver beet, then season to taste with salt and pepper.

Snapper

Season the skin side of the snapper with salt and cook in butter, until it is 80 per cent cooked through on this side. Turn and cook for the last 20 per cent. The skin should be nice and crispy and the flesh juicy.

To serve

Place some of the potato sauté in the middle of each plate. Place a snapper fillet on top and drizzle the kina sauce around. Top the fish with salsa verde and garnish the plate with more kina roe and fresh herbs and olive oil.

ZUPPA DI PESCE ALLA SICILIANA (SICILIAN FISH SOUP)

LUCA VILLARI, AL VOLO PIZZERIA
SERVES 2–4

100 ml virgin olive oil
2 cloves garlic, finely
  chopped
1 pinch saffron threads
1 punnet cherry tomatoes
4 sprigs thyme
1 pinch chilli flakes
50 g pitted green olives,
  sliced
2 tablespoons chopped
  capers
salt and pepper, to taste
100 ml white wine
2 cups fish stock
1 cup tomato passata
1 kg fresh mixed seafood
  (this can be whatever you
  can source fresh: white
  fish, mussels, cockles,
  squid, scallops, etc.)

Sofrito topping
virgin olive oil
2 cloves garlic, finely
  chopped
2–3 tablespoons chopped
  flat-leaf parsley
zest of ½ lemon

Italian food is very simple. It's fresh, it's vibrant, it's tasty and we don't like to complicate things. I'm a firm believer that when it comes to cooking, never use cheap wine. If it's good enough for me to drink, its good enough to go in my food, and the rest — well, that's for socialising time, because you know what? Socialising is very important to us Sicilians.'

— Luca Villari

Stir-fry all the soup ingredients together except the wine, stock, passata and seafood. Deglaze the pan with the wine and add the other liquids.

Bring to the boil, adding in all fish and shellfish. Simmer gently until shellfish have opened.

To make the sofrito, stir-fry all ingredients for 1–2 minutes.

Serve in warmed bowls and top with sofrito mix.

6

MALAYSIAN SAILS

LOCATION
**ROMPIN DISTRICT,
MALAYSIA**

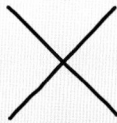

✕

FISH OF THE DAY
**SAILFISH AND
GIANT GOURAMI**

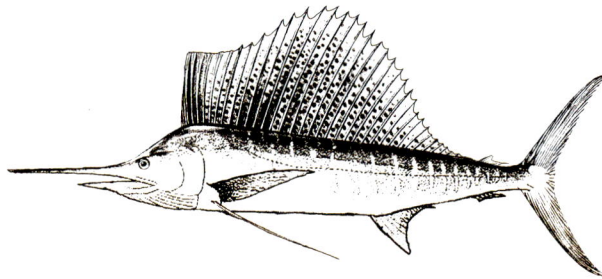

W ho knew Malaysia had a thriving game-fishing scene? Who knew Malaysia had tigers that stalk people fishing on riverbanks? These two things I learned the easy and then the hard way on a trip through this incredible part of the world.

Malaysia is home to the oldest rainforests on Earth — forests that are alive with monkeys, elephants and tigers. Its coastal towns bustle with a rich diversity of culture and its markets overflow with produce, fresh fish and friendly people. But I wasn't there for a holiday — I went to fulfil a childhood dream, to catch one of the most spectacular game fish on the planet.

I had never associated the South China Sea with game fishing, and yet here off the coast of Malaysia's Rompin District was a thriving sailfish population. Sailfish are one of the fishing world's ultimate catches, and fishers travel the world to chase them. Unusually, off the coast here they gather in big numbers in shallow waters for what must be a spawning aggregation.

Previous spread
The beach in front of Tioman Cabana and the Rumah Hijau conservation centre on Tioman Island, Malaysia.

Today the sailfish are protected, the area designated a catch-and-release-only fishery — one fiercely preserved by local fishermen who realised that far more money could be made by taking people out each day for an experience, than just removing the lot. The customers who lined the wharves that morning were a testament to this smarter way to value the resource — providing enjoyment and sustainable economic gain to many. The entire fishing industry here is powered by the addiction to game fishing that has swept through China. We were one of just a handful of non-Chinese groups fishing that day.

My mission here was not just to catch a sailfish, but to catch one on a popper or a stick bait. I headed off on a longboat handmade probably just metres from the wharf, fashioned in wood cut from trees like the ones we passed heading down the river and out to sea. My guide spoke almost no English and our skipper spoke none.

The fleet, probably 30 or so boats, were all headed to the same spot. First we had a shallow fish for live baits, before all descending on an area probably only 5 or 10 km square. As boat after boat hooked sailfish up on live baits, I kept casting my popper at the throng of surface-feeding sails that surrounded us. At one stage there would have been eight or ten sailfish all airborne on the ends of lines around us at the same time. Finally I hooked up, only for the fish to leap clear out of the water and spit my popper high into the air in disgust.

Never give up! A few hours and many, many casts later, a follow, a strike and the hooks were set to the most aerial fish I have ever had on the end of a line. Run after run, my spinning reel drag got the workout of a lifetime. Then just when I had it beat, too much vertical pressure saw my rod break clean in half! Somehow, though, I got my fish to the boat, held it up for the obligatory 'man and fish' picture before releasing it back into the briny, ready for the next eager angler to have a crack.

I have indelible memories of finishing the day's fishing trip in a precarious shack on a wonky wharf, itself a ramshackle restaurant with gaps in the floorboards looking to the water below. Inside, a busy open

kitchen bustled with chefs slicing up fish fresh off the boats while plucky cats stalked around, trying their luck. The tables around us were full of visiting fishermen, almost all from China, shirts lifted over exposed bellies, excitedly reliving the day's successes and losses in a language completely new to me. And although I couldn't understand the words, the hand gestures and facial expressions were from a universal fishing language, easy to understand. Next to us were two large (I'll take a guess) Russian gentlemen, accompanied by ladies on the clock, with all parties exhaling clouds of tobacco smoke that engulfed the entire restaurant, creating an atmosphere that felt more like a movie set than real life.

A few hours and many, many casts later, a follow, a strike and I was hooked up to the most aerial fish I have ever had on the end of a line.

The food here was sensational — plates of fried squid legs with a crisp brown batter to rival the Colonel, woks of steaming unidentifiable vegetables, beautiful sauces and dishes of rice, all complementing seafood caught just hours before and now served super-fresh with beer in huge bottles — enjoyed while looking over a tropical estuary with a dirty, hazy 30°C sunset in the background and 1000 per cent humidity. It was an experience for all the senses. I will never forget the scene — all it needed was for Jason Statham to wander in and start a bar fight.

The next day we made a visit to a little island called Tioman. Tioman is to the Malaysians what the Barrier Reef is to Australians. It sits about 30 km out in the South China Sea, and not only has one of the most biodiverse coral reef systems on Earth but, on land, its rainforests are home to an incredible diversity of mammals and birds. A hundred and thirty-eight different bird species to be exact, and when it comes to mammals, the most common here is without question the tourist.

Tioman's beaches starred as Bali Hai in the 1958 movie *South Pacific*, and *Time* magazine named Tioman as one of the world's most beautiful islands. Now it is Malaysia's most popular tourist destination. But I

Opposite above
The sailfish charter fleet sits waiting for its guests in the early morning light, Kuala Rompin, Malaysia.

Opposite below
After casting unsuccessfully for most of the day, I finally catch and release my first sailfish on a popper.

wanted to visit for other reasons: to look at a recycling programme run by the locals and to have a few dives on the island's unique coral reef.

I met up with Raden al Haziq from Reef Check Malaysia to look at the work of the Rumah Hijau conservation centre. Two amazing ideas that stood out for me were the repurposing of single-use plastic bags — heated, pressed and turned into everything from purses to aprons and sold back to the tourists — and grinding up glass bottles to supply to the building trade, to reduce the amount of sand being taken from the beaches to be used as substrate for concrete.

'We need to educate people, especially local islanders, to improve their lifestyle by inventing or innovating things from their waste material like plastic. This way, rather than just seeing it as a problem, we create solutions,' Raden says. 'We need more people to realise that their contribution to save our environment is really important.'

You can stay at the Rumah Hijau conservation centre and get involved in their work, with accommodation in beachfront villas constructed from recycled glass bottles. What amazed me about Raden and his team was just how much they were achieving from such a small centre amongst the throng of visiting tourists — a wee glimmer of what we can accomplish when we set our minds to protecting the environment.

Then I got to dive. To be honest, I wasn't expecting much given the volume of divers that descend on the coral reefs here daily, but I was pleasantly surprised. The reefs were stunning, with turtles, a myriad of fish and what I'd really come to see, the incredible diversity of corals. When you spend time diving in reef systems around the world you get to appreciate all the differences, great and small, so I speak with confidence when I say that Tioman is up there with the best I've ever experienced.

The last part of my adventure here took us inland. It was time to change it up and go freshwater.

'We need to educate people to improve their lifestyle by inventing or innovating things from their waste material like plastic. We need more people to realise that their contribution to save our environment is really important.'

— RADEN AL HAZIQ, REEF CHECK MALAYSIA

Now, I'd hazard a guess that I'd be one of only a tiny and elite club that has been stalked by a tiger while fishing. This table-turning Malaysian experience highlighted just how far we were from our Kiwi comfort zone, where our only large-cat threat is the mystery black panther of Canterbury.

Now, to be fair we had put ourselves into a position far out of the ordinary. We had been invited deep into the Endau-Rompin National Park to fish a river surrounded by the world's oldest rainforest, a sprightly 130 million years young.

Our guides tracked us into the jungle past great piles of fresh elephant dung to the edge of a rich, brown river, surrounded by lush, damp jungle. Suddenly one guide shot up his arm, a universal signal to stand still and be quiet. He pointed out a tiger on the far bank, and we could all hear it as it slipped behind the bush line, 'chuffing' while moving towards us. Then it went dead quiet, which was much, much worse, the nearby birds shrieking their alerts and barking deer making us extremely aware that we still had company.

Staring across a river perhaps just 20 m wide, knowing that at that moment we were being watched by one of the world's greatest predators, is a feeling not easily forgotten. From the way the guides made us form a tight group and posted lookouts forwards and back, it was obvious they were taking this extremely seriously. I needed my fish and I needed it fast.

As dusk approached and our very nervous guides anxiously told us through translators that it was time to leave, I was never going to utter the usual 'just one more cast' line. Luckily, at that exact moment we hooked our dinner — a solid and very edible giant gourami. This is a fish more commonly seen in aquariums than on the plate, but with the skills of Shyleena, a flamboyant local chef, all the flavours of Malaysia came together to finish off a stunning adventure.

Previous spread
A resting green sea turtle in Tioman's coral reef.

MASAK SANTAN LEMAK IKAN CILI CEKUR

SHYLEENA FARIDAH HOPE
SERVES 6

1.5 kg fresh fish (we used ikan kaloi/giant gourami)
8 nodes of turmeric
6 stalks lemongrass
salt
1 banana leaf
3 pieces fresh ginger
6 cloves garlic
5 rhizomes cekur (sand ginger, *Kaempferia galanga* — if unable to find, use extra-fresh ginger)
10 leaves cekur (sand ginger, *Kaempferia galanga* — if unable to find, use 2 pieces of turmeric leaf)
20 g belacan (shrimp paste)
6 small red onions or 4 large
4 whole large red chillies
4 whole large green chillies
3 tablespoons cooking oil
2 cups water
2 cups coconut milk
10 belimbing buluh fruit (sorrel tree, *Averrhoa bilimbi* — if unable to find, use 2 slices of lemon)
brown sugar
3 stalks coriander, for garnish

Fish preparation

Clean the fish and remove scales but leave the skin on. Cut fish into equal-size portions, approximately 200 g each. Place on a tray.

Seasoning

Peel 4 pieces of turmeric and place in the mortar along with 3 stalks of lemongrass cut into 10 cm lengths. Add one dessertspoon of salt (or to taste). Grind ingredients with the pestle until they become a lumpy paste. Rub the seasoning onto the skin of all the pieces of fish. Cover the fish with a banana leaf if available, or other cover. For best flavour, place the tray in the fridge for half an hour.

Sauce

Peel all the ginger, garlic, cekur rhizomes and the other 4 pieces of turmeric, and place into the mortar, along with 3 stalks of lemongrass cut into 10 cm lengths. Add in 5 leaves of cekur and 20 g shrimp paste. Cut the onions and red and green chillies into small pieces and add into the mortar. Use the pestle to grind the ingredients into a lumpy paste (this may take a few minutes).

Fish cooking

Place a wok over a high heat and add the cooking oil. Wait until the oil is hot, then place 2 pieces of fish at a time in the oil. Cook for 1 minute on each side, remove and place on a tray. When all the fish is cooked, cover the tray with banana leaf or other cover.

Add the sauce into the wok and cook until mixture is slightly golden in colour. Add water and 5 chopped leaves of cekur. Bring mixture to a simmer, then add coconut milk. Bring to a simmer again and wait for 2 minutes before adding all the fish and the belimbing buluh.

Cover the wok with a banana leaf (or wok lid) and cook for 15–20 minutes, until the fish is cooked all the way through. Add salt and brown sugar to taste.

Place fish and sauce onto plates, and decorate with coriander and thin strips of chilli.

7

THE THIRD ISLAND

LOCATION
**STEWART ISLAND,
NEW ZEALAND**

✕

FISH OF THE DAY
TRUMPETER

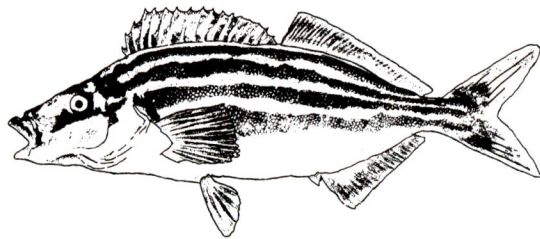

If you know one of those people who always promises to catch up with friends yet rarely does, then you'll know exactly how Stewart Island feels. Most Kiwis have it down as a 'must visit' destination, but the vast majority of us never find the time.

Not that I think Stewart Island minds much at all. At 19 times the size of Waiheke Island, it is New Zealand's third largest island, but with a population of just two full Waiheke ferries. It's a place that does just fine without the polar-fleeced hordes descending en masse.

Stewart Island/Rakiura lies in one of the most challenging stretches of water on the planet. Sitting in the infamous Roaring Forties, it is surrounded by freezing Southern Ocean water and home to unpredictable ocean currents and giant, man-eating sharks. These waters sink more commercial boats that almost any other place in New Zealand. Why? Because of our insatiable appetite for the seafood this dangerous body of water is home to: pāua, crayfish, blue cod and the iconic and arguably best wild oysters on the planet — Bluff oysters.

Being so far south, it gets dark early and light late during winter, and

Previous spread
Of all the islands surrounding Stewart Island, this is by far the most dangerous. Motunui/Edwards Island is a hotspot for some of the biggest great white sharks on Earth.

the long twilights over summer make the days seem never-ending. Only in Antarctica have I seen a sunset and sunrise take as long as it does here. It's an eerie elongated dusk, which in the winter seems to start at about 4 p.m., perfectly complementing the brooding mood of this isolated place.

There's not just the one island. From the smaller outer islands covered in flapping muttonbirds, to the success story of our awkward flightless kākāpō on Whenua Hou; to Motunui/Edwards Island, visited by seasonal great white sharks; or Ulva Island's bird sanctuary, Stewart Island is an oasis for an abundance of endangered wildlife. And the island's human locals are fierce kaitiaki or guardians of these taonga or treasures.

Ulva Island is New Zealand's southernmost bird sanctuary. Most of it has never been milled, making its forest amongst the most pristine in the country. On top of this, it's been pest-free since 1997, the resulting populations of birds showing visitors just how much impact our introduced mammals have had on our vulnerable native bird populations almost everywhere else. The only place I've heard birdsong like I did here is on Little Barrier Island in the Hauraki Gulf, also a sanctuary. A visit to Ulva is a must-do here, and is just a seven-minute water-taxi trip from the main town, Oban.

Another must-do is a trip to Motunui/Edwards Island, to see what is one of only a handful of great white shark hotspots on Earth. The sharks here are lauded by scientists and filmmakers as some of the biggest and most aggressive on the planet. Here, on an average summer day, you can see up to half a dozen of these 3 to 6 m long formidable ocean predators coming within centimetres of the boat. It can also be just centimetres from your mask if you're brave enough to get into the freezing Southern Ocean in the shark cage to take a look. The shark season runs from December through to around May/June and it is bucket-list stuff.

Birds were a constant companion on our trip down to this hidden corner of New Zealand, from the albatross surrounding our boat every time we stopped, to the kākā that sat on the railing outside our accommodation, to the kiwi that roam freely at night. In fact, so common are kiwi here that

you can spy them everywhere from the local rugby pitch at dusk to down on the beach digging for and eating sand hoppers around your feet. Seeing our national bird through squinty eyes in a dark enclosure at the zoo is one thing, but spying two in the wild having a massive scrap on the side of the local airstrip, as we did with our guide from Beaks and Feathers, is something else entirely. Before visiting Stewart Island I never knew how fast these woolly-looking drumsticks could move. I can tell you that, in the wild, our national bird has some serious pace.

'They're very family-orientated birds, these kiwi, very territorial,' our guide, Matt Jones, tells us. 'They can get very stroppy with each other regarding territories and you see some pretty fearsome fighting.

'Females have got that call like somebody's getting murdered. Imagine if you were in the dark with no torch — it sounds like a zombie coming for you, it's quite a horrific sound. The male makes a quite high-pitched whistle kind of sound — it's quite distinctive.'

Birds aside, for a person of the ocean Stewart Island exerts an extra pull. I've been lucky enough to dive in most places around our beautiful country, and I can tell you that underwater here is unlike anywhere else.

Diving down through huge kelp forests, with shafts of light radiating down from the green above, the variety of marine life is astonishing. Fish you don't often see in other places gather in the shallows in good numbers: trumpeter, blue moki, copper moki, blue cod, red cod, tarakihi. Then there's octopus, crayfish, pāua thick on the rocks and kina the size of dinner plates everywhere. The temperature of the water here proves no barrier to a flourishing of life; quite the opposite, the cold seems to encourage it.

Our target fish here was trumpeter. For the first two days, all we caught was blue cod — hundreds of them. Surrounded by hungry albatross, getting the fish back in the water without them getting swallowed whole by monster hungry birds was an exercise in itself.

On the third day, underwater footage from our dives had showed us that the trumpeter were sitting higher than usual in the water column, so we tried fishing midwater and straight away our luck changed. By lunchtime we had a few good trumpeter in the boat, then a quick snorkel in the

Diving down through huge kelp forests, with shafts of light tangling in the green above, the variety of marine life is astonishing.

Opposite above
You know you are in the Roaring Forties when the trees grow like this.

Opposite below
From forests above to forests below. Heading into the kelp in search of pāua.

shallows provided more than enough huge pāua to complete our meal. Then it was back to the South Sea Hotel for our last night on the island.

If you don't fly to the island, you have to get there by boat from Bluff, across the infamous Foveaux Strait, one of our more notorious stretches of water. The strait's deepest point is less than 30 m and, with monster currents and a ton of wind and swell spun up from the Roaring Forties, wave heights often exceed 10 m — large mountains of water which suddenly stand to attention with little warning. The crossing is a literal rite of passage, which makes a safe arrival into harbour on either side all the more satisfying.

It is a journey that is guided by a single voice, a beacon of reassurance, like the bright beam from a lighthouse guiding you away from danger. Meri Leask is the voice of the fisherman's VHF radio down here, and at the start of every journey and its completion she's there to check you in or welcome you home. Meri has been there for the worst of the worst, when Foveaux unleashes hell and all a fisherman has is her reassuring voice.

She guided us out of Bluff on our journey across in search of adventure and trumpeter, and she guided us home with a storm close behind. On our way back, we were accompanied into port by a fleet of oystermen.

As well as giant waves, Foveaux Strait is famous for one of New Zealand's most iconic seafoods: the Bluff oyster. Every year, when the season is open from 1 March till the end of August, these brave men and women head to sea to harvest this delicacy from the inhospitable and volatile waters of the strait. Every year becomes increasingly difficult; while the boats today are far more seaworthy than those of their grandfathers, the same improvement has not been seen in the oyster beds, which are tired after years of dredging. Unstable oyster numbers are putting increased pressure on families, on communities and on ecosystems.

Stewart Island is home to some of our most incredible wildlife and some of our best conservation success stories on land. At sea, however, we have work to do to ensure that those who live and make a living in this hidden paradise may enjoy doing so for generations to come.

> **Surrounded by hungry albatross, getting the cod back in the water without them getting swallowed whole by monster hungry birds was an exercise in itself.**

Previous spread, clockwise from top left
A huge octopus I found on my hunt for pāua; *Fish of the Day's* Jeanneau 895 heads out from Bluff into the Foveaux Strait; One of many albatross encountered at Stewart Island — the Buller's mollymawk; Often the hardest part about soft baiting for fat blue cod is getting past all the ravenous smaller ones; Using a plastic trowel to pry pāua off the rocks so as not to hurt them — pāua are haemophiliacs; The catch — huge New Zealand pāua and kina.

Opposite above
A night walk around Oban will reward you with sights like this — New Zealand's southern brown kiwi.

Opposite below
A sneaky visit by the tax man, in this case a 4 m great white shark. No diving today.

CRISPY-SKINNED TRUMPETER WITH PĀUA BONBONS AND SMOKED BLUFF OYSTERS

SIMON HENRY, ASCOT PARK HOTEL, INVERCARGILL
SERVES 6

Bluff oyster sauce

1 litre water
1 dozen shucked, pottled Bluff oysters and oyster liquid
2 teaspoons white sugar
2 teaspoons soy sauce
½ teaspoon arrowroot powder

Smoked Bluff oysters

1 dozen Bluff oysters, reserved from oyster sauce recipe
30 ml soy sauce
mānuka wood chips

Pāua bonbons

1 cup minced pāua
½ small onion, diced
80 g lean bacon, diced
1 tablespoon chopped parsley
½ clove garlic, crushed
2 eggs
200 g plain flour
salt and pepper
200 ml milk
500 g breadcrumbs

Crispy-skinned trumpeter

2 large fillets of trumpeter, boned, with skin left on
50 ml clarified butter
50 ml canola oil
salt and pepper

Lightly pickled cucumber

1 small telegraph cucumber, sliced thinly lengthways
¼ cup white wine vinegar
1 teaspoon sugar
¾ teaspoon crushed red chilli flakes

Bluff oyster sauce

Add the water to a pot and heat to a light simmer. Add the oysters and the oyster liquid to the pot and lightly simmer (but do not boil) for 20 minutes, stirring occasionally.

Remove the oysters from the pot and reserve. Strain the remaining liquid through a muslin cloth and return to the stove over a low heat. Reduce the liquid to 100 ml or one-tenth of its original volume.

Add the sugar and the soy sauce, stirring to dissolve the sugar. Mix the arrowroot with a little water and slowly add to the oyster sauce to slightly thicken. Taste and adjust seasoning if required.

Smoked Bluff oysters

Place the oysters on a baking rack and lightly brush with soy sauce. Prepare your smoker with mānuka wood chips and cold-smoke the bluff oysters for 15 minutes, ensuring you don't cook the oysters further. When the oysters are smoked, place them in the fridge until needed.

Pāua bonbons

Place pāua, onion, bacon, parsley, garlic, 1 egg and 50 g of flour in a bowl. Season with salt and pepper and mix to combine.

Roll the pāua mixture into small balls around 3 cm in diameter, and place in the fridge to set for half an hour.

Place the remaining flour in a bowl and season with salt and pepper. To a second bowl add the other egg and the milk, and whisk till well combined. To a third bowl add the breadcrumbs.

To crumb the pāua bonbons, place a few at a time into the flour, coating lightly. Secondly, place them in the egg wash, covering them completely, then roll them in the crumb mix. Double-crumb each bonbon by repeating stages two and three. Set aside in the fridge until needed.

Crispy-skinned trumpeter

Pat each fillet dry with paper towels. Cut each fillet into 3 portions. Turn each fish portion skin-side up and lightly score by just cutting

2 teaspoons kosher salt
2 tablespoons chopped dill
2 tablespoons lemon juice

Garnish
sea chicory
cuttlefish ink
dill

100 ml canola oil, for frying

through the skin of each portion a few times. This will help the ends of the portions of fish to not roll up when cooking. Season generously.

Place a heavy-based frying pan over a medium heat and add the clarified butter and canola oil. When the oil is hot and slightly smoking, place the trumpeter portions skin-side down in the pan. Cook for 3–4 minutes or until golden brown, then flip and cook the other side for a further 3–4 minutes, until cooked through. Remove the cooked fillets from the pan and let them rest on paper towels to absorb any excess oil. Season lightly with salt and pepper.

Lightly pickled cucumber
Add the cucumber and all other ingredients to a large bowl, then toss lightly and let stand for 10 minutes before serving.

To serve
Hydrate the sea chicory in water and let it stand for 5 minutes. Lightly heat the Bluff oyster sauce and smoked Bluff oysters, using a little of the oyster sauce to coat the smoked oysters.

Fry the pāua bonbons in a heavy-based pan in 100 ml of canola oil until lightly golden brown, then finish in a moderate oven for 8–10 minutes.

Place an artistic line or two of cuttlefish ink on the plate, followed by another couple of lines of warmed Bluff oyster sauce. Add a cooked portion of trumpeter, skin-side up and place 3 pāua bonbons around it. Finally, roll up 3 pickled cucumber ribbons and place them between the bonbons. Place 2 smoked Bluff oysters on each plate and garnish with sea chicory and dill.

8

LEARNING BISLAMA

LOCATION
VANUATU

FISH OF THE DAY
DOGTOOTH TUNA

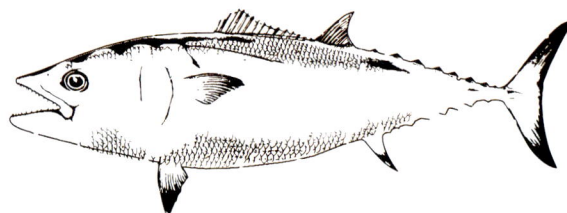

You've been to Fiji, holidayed in Rarotonga and visited Samoa, so now you think you've got a handle on the Pacific. Well, can I present to you Vanuatu, a place that will totally reset what you think a Pacific island can be, and open up endless new opportunities to explore.

Let's start with the name, Vanuatu, which translated into English means 'our land forever'. Renamed after gaining its independence in 1980 (it was formerly called the New Hebrides), 'Vanuatu' perfectly captures this rich and diverse group of islands. There are 83 islands in total, with such a diverse collection of Melanesian peoples that they speak over 110 distinctly different languages, as well as French and English. To bridge the local language difference almost everyone here also speaks a universal dialect called Bislama, a type of pidgin English.

From one end of the island group to the other, the people look different, talk different and do remarkably different things. From the land-diving ni-Vanuatu of Pentecost Island, the original bungy jumpers; to the water-slapping women of Gaua, who use their cupped hands to create music with

Previous spread
The idyllic Champagne Beach on Espiritu Santo Island in Northern Vanuatu.

water; to the volcanic island of Tanna, where the strongest kava in the whole of the Pacific comes from, this place is an adventurer's paradise. Due to the topography of the reefs surrounding the islands, the fishery is still in relatively good condition, as foreign trawlers and longliners have been unable to fish it to any great degree until recently.

If history gets you up early to slide into your jandals, there are several rich veins here to pursue: from local cultures and customs, thousands of years in the making, to the indelible impact of World War II. I was lucky enough to travel to Espiritu Santo to wreck-dive the largest accessible sunken liner in the world, the SS *President Coolidge*, a 200 m long wreck lying on her side not far from where she hit friendly mines. I was even luckier (or not, depending on the level of adrenaline you are up for) to experience an underwater earthquake when I was 20 m below the surface, finning into the wreck. The short, sharp, localised shake had a dark, violent, throbbing effect. It compressed my body in such a way that for a moment I assumed I had the bends. With the quake stirring the sediment inside the wreck, it was possible to continue guided only by the beam of my torch. Now that was truly living!

And if wreck-diving is your dive-ticket, then you will probably already know of the famous Million Dollar Point. After World War II, a heap of military equipment sat idle, deployed here by the US for defence and the building of runways, being too expensive to ship back home. Disgruntled that they couldn't sell it to the British and French administrators of the islands, even for just a few cents in the dollar, the Americans chose to build a temporary wharf on the edge of the coral reef and literally drove everything off it into the deep water below.

The term 'million-dollar' seems quaint by today's standards, as untold amounts of trucks, trailers, jeeps, water tanks, graders and military gear was sent to its watery demise. There are even huge D9 bulldozers lying end to end where they landed perfectly on top of each other. Thankfully today Vanuatu is getting a return on the Americans' stubbornness by way of tourists paying good money to come and dive this huge underwater tip.

Aside from the diving, I came to this vast archipelago to chase my

nemesis: the dogtooth tuna. I call it my nemesis because it's the fish that once very nearly drowned me.

I was spearfishing for dogtooth in Niue a few years earlier and managed to spear one in around 30 m of water — absolutely at the edge of my range as a free-diver. As I began my ascent up the line from my spear to my surface float, the swivel that attaches the line to the float failed. I watched as the end of the line came racing past me as my dogtooth headed for the depths.

Instinctively, I grabbed it — I didn't want to lose this fish of a lifetime. Bad move! Suddenly I was back down around 20 m, battling the huge fish and absolutely out of breath. Realising my mistake, I let go and headed for the surface, but I didn't quite make it, blacking out in the last few metres.

> **I call the dogtooth tuna my nemesis because it's the fish that once very nearly drowned me.**

Shallow-water blackouts like the one I experienced are responsible for a lot of free-diving deaths. Luckily for me I had a very attentive buddy, Brendon Pasisi, who grabbed me at the surface and saved my life. Thanks, Brendon! Ever since then, getting a dogtooth has become an obsession and this trip was my chance. My aim was to get one on spear, and one on rod and reel.

We travelled from Santo back down through the islands to Port Vila on the liveaboard fishing charter boat *Nambas*, a Black Watch 40. Our host Russ Housby is one of the best charter operators in the business, and a specialist when it comes to dogtooth, boasting an array of world records for these incredibly elusive fish. Russ has been based out of Havannah Harbour on the island of Efate for the past 15 years, and not only is he a bloody good skipper, he also cooks like a Michelin-star chef.

'Catching dogtooth is no easy task,' he warned us. 'First you've got to find them, then get the bite, then hook 'em. You need to be able to free-spool the bait nicely and cleanly, and not allow the fish to know you are there. If they feel the slightest bit of tension, generally they will drop the bait.'

'Then once you have hooked them, you've still got to survive the reef and potentially the sharks, so there are a lot of challenges to actually catch that fish and put 'em in the boat.'

As we began our journey south, we dragged plastic across the vast mirror-calm expanses of ocean between the reefs and islands. This produced an array of pelagics from mahimahi to blue marlin, and we didn't have long to wait between bites.

All along the way there was evidence of remote villages, where islanders were still subsistence-living with no power and very little contact with the outside world. We anchored one evening off the isolated island of Malekula, arms weary from fighting fish all day. As the sun dithered on the horizon, the pulsing glow of nearby Mount Ambrym's volcanic lava lake, the size of four football fields, smeared a red-fire reflection on the clouds above.

Just staying in the boat became an artform, as the fish regularly pulled me hard to the gunwales.

As if on cue, several young boys from the local village paddled out in a hand-carved canoe and bartered boatside under the volcanic orange sunset. 'Mister, mister, banana, mister?', a bunch of fresh bananas becoming currency traded for a packet of biscuits. Off they paddled into the failing light, happy with their special treat, unknowingly providing an even richer experience for those of us on board, who in that moment felt such a long, long way from home.

On we travelled, still chasing that dogtooth tuna. Just south of Norsup on Malekula we finally hooked up and the battle began. And a battle royale it was indeed. Russ had reset my drag to apply around 24 kg of pressure when we needed it, and within a few minutes he was ordering me to crank it up. 'All the way forward, mate — need you to man up for me!' came the cry from the bridge deck.

At this much pressure while standing on a bouncing deck, just staying in the boat became an artform, as the fish regularly pulled me hard to the

Opposite above
Waiting for a bite as the sun sets on day 4 of my hunt for the dogtooth tuna.

Opposite below
With Laura MacLucas and a couple of solid dogtooth tuna hooked and landed at the eleventh hour.

gunwales. Then, just as we had the fish to the boat, the hook straightened and it fell off. I can't remember ever feeling that much disappointment. Bugger.

From there we headed down to the Maskelyne Islands, then across to Epi and down to Emae, fishing and spearfishing all the way. Pelagic after pelagic dragged us to our next bottom-fishing spot. Here we paused, and every drop we hooked up. An array of deep-reef species like giant red bass and coral trout came up from the depths. I used these stops to jump in with the speargun in the hope of finding a doggie within range of my gun, but to no avail. My fish of the day was proving far more difficult to get than I ever thought.

Finally we headed to our last location, the steep walls off the island of Makura. I had to make the choice: jump in with the spear and risk it all or try with rod and reel. With a little encouragement from the bridge deck, we chose to use up our final hours with the latter.

True to form, just a half-hour before we had to head back to Vila, we got onto them. Suddenly, we were dealing with a double hook-up, with Russ's partner Laura showing us an alternative use for a jandal. Every fisherman knows the pain of having the end of a rod placed in the groin area while you fight a large fish, if you either don't have a gimbal belt to use or just forget to strap it on before the fight gets too intense. Laura had the answer. Minutes into the fight she took off one of her jandals and slipped it into her pants to provide the perfect cushioning. The fish we were hooked up to were really pulling hard, and Russ had his work cut out getting us off the reef and into deeper water.

The length of the battle and the way the fish ran suggested we might have the right species on the end of our lines. Finally, after a huge effort, the fish came to the boat — both solid dogtooth. All that was required now was Russ's prowess in the kitchen to finish an incredible journey through a little-known part of the world. Getting my nemesis with a speargun would have to wait for another day.

SEARED TATAKI DOGTOOTH TUNA WITH KECAP MANIS SAUCE

RUSS HOUSBY
SERVES 4

1 kg fresh dogtooth tuna
   fillets
sesame oil
black pepper
200 g brown sugar
300 ml soy sauce
   (Kikkoman or any other
   good-quality soy)
wasabi mayo
mayonnaise
wasabi, to taste
zest of 1 lemon
pinch each of salt and
   pepper

Cut the tuna fillets to create 7–8 cm square-shaped lengths, then roll them in sesame oil and cover in fresh ground black pepper. Sear the fish on a hot skillet, until just the outside layer is coloured.

Take the fillets and wrap them in paper towels to remove the excess oil. While still in the paper towels, wrap in aluminium foil, then place into a freezer to chill.

To make the kecap manis sauce (soy reduction), mix the brown sugar and soy sauce together in a saucepan. Place over a low heat and reduce until it becomes syrupy. Transfer to a squirt bottle and leave to cool.

Mix together the wasabi mayo, mayonnaise and wasabi (to taste), then add lemon zest, and salt and pepper. Add more wasabi if required, then transfer into a squirt bottle and refrigerate.

To serve

Remove the fish from the freezer and unwrap. Gently slice the fillet down the squared roll, making each cut just a few millimetres thick. Lay these out to cover a plate.

Take the kecap manis in the squirt bottle and paint lines across the fish, making a straight line pattern. Turn the plate ninety degrees and use the wasabi mayo squirt bottle to repeat the process, to make a grid pattern.

9

THE DREAM STREAM

LOCATION
**ROTORUA,
NEW ZEALAND**

✕

FISH OF THE DAY
BROWN TROUT

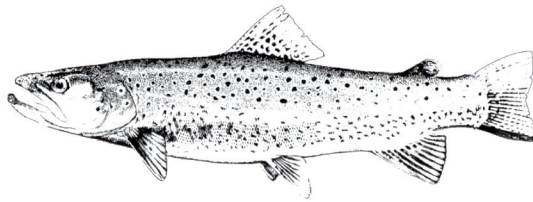

Fishing author Harry Middleton once said: 'Fishing is not an escape from life, but often a deeper immersion into it.' Patiently waiting for my chance here on this stream as the fish of my dreams glide effortlessly by, I must agree. I'd heard whispers of this place, this fly fisherman's nirvana; fishing yarns spoken softly in dark corners of riverside taverns. And now I had been given the chance to fish one of the best trout streams on the planet.

The words 'Dream Stream' conjure up all sorts of ideas in your head. Over the weeks leading up to my trip to Rotorua, I had started building a picture of what I thought this place would be like, in much the same way that you put faces to the characters of books you've read. The problem with this type of visualisation is the disappointment that follows the release of the movie version, when those characters, so clear in your mind's eye, are represented by actors who look nothing like those you had imagined. So it was with the Dream Stream — the stories I had heard about it were not helping. Fishermen's accounts often grow bigger and more fanciful as time goes by, and my expectations were, like those stories, becoming larger

Previous spread
The iconic 'Dream Stream', one of Rotorua's best-kept secrets.

than life. How could this place possibly live up to all the hype?

We arrived in Rotorua early. With me I had chef Anthony McNamara, a keen fly fisher himself. Before we headed to the Dream Stream, I wanted to take Anthony to another equally impressive bit of water: the Kaituna, which flows north out of lakes Rotorua and Rotoiti. But we weren't fishing this time: I wanted to take Anthony over the world's highest commercially rafted waterfall. Known as the Tutea falls, it's a 7 metre plunge, pushing 18 tonnes of water a second through a narrow cut in the steep rock walls. It's 50:50 as to whether the raft lands you upright at the end or spits you into the pool upside down. We landed right way up, this time.

But despite all the thrills, there was still our secret destination, a river purportedly so full of trout that their backs glisten in the sun as they stick out above the surface of the water on the stream's shallow gravel runs. To get there and to secure access you need a guide, and a good one. Thankfully Miles Rushmer was one such person.

Miles is good, real good, and his gift of the gab means he's managed to talk his way into accessing places like the Dream Stream. But it's not only this place — Miles has a bunch of picture-postcard spots hidden deep in the bush that produce fish American anglers would die for. He's been fishing these parts for over 35 years, and guiding for around 20 of those.

He's got a big reputation as a stalking specialist and knows how to get you into casting range in some of the clearest streams and rivers around. Then there's that dry humour. It's hard to not come away from a Rushmer trip without a big smile, a ton of stories to try to recount and one or two very good fish landed.

But there was a catch — Miles had promised to take us in to the Dream Stream, but not actually reveal where it was. So, with blindfolds on, we were loaded into his 4WD to begin the trip. This sensory deprivation again allowed my mind to start visualising what this spot would be like. As it turned out, on arrival, the 'movie version' was a near-perfect match to the depiction of the 'book' in my head.

The landowners allow only a few anglers access to the stream each

It's hard to not come away from a Miles Rushmer trip without a big smile, a ton of stories to try to recount and one or two bloody good fish landed.

season, and in the past it has been booked out years in advance by foreign fly fishers searching for that ultimate experience. As a small silver lining to the new world we live in, Kiwis are now getting an opportunity to experience more of their own backyard. Plenty have been using expert guides like Miles not just to fish places like the Dream Stream, but to access the thousands of other fishing opportunities this area is renowned for, both in rivers and lakes.

As I mentioned back in chapter one, a freshwater angler's ultimate is a trout weighing 10 pounds (4.5 kg) or more. Catching a 10-pounder is entirely achievable with the right combination of guide, season, skill and of course, lady luck. Known as a 'double-figure fish', they can be found in this stream full of mainly big fat brown trout.

Rainbow trout are also prevalent in Rotorua waters, some of them fattening themselves up on native freshwater crayfish, earning the nickname 'kōura munchers'. These fish are desirable for their eating qualities, as the oil-rich kōura cause the flesh of the trout to go bright orange and take on a superior, crayfish-like taste.

I wanted to catch one of those for Anthony to cook up, but first I wanted to see if I could finally join that double-figure club. I'd come close in back-country Fiordland, but not close enough. If I was going to do it anywhere in the North Island, it was going to be here.

The first fish we stalked up behind turned out to be a brown over 8 pounds in weight, but not quite the 10 I was looking for. It was impressive how close Miles got me to the fish. Slowly working our way up behind it in the fish's blindspot, literally all I had to do was drop the nymph on its nose from the tip of my 6-weight fly rod.

'Strike!' came the call from Miles, and then all hell broke loose as the fish made a beeline for the safety of an overhanging willow tree. There were logs and branches everywhere, and I literally had to run after the fish to keep side pressure on, dragging it away from certain disaster. Once we were clear of all the nasty stuff, I was able to steer the fish into the shallows and Miles's waiting net. Hook out and away the big jack went, as all browns are released here.

Next it was Anthony's turn, hooking up and landing a solid rainbow that was also released. Then another brown for me. This one was hiding under a log. With some valuable guiding tips from Miles, again we were able to keep the fish away from danger, and within a few minutes it was safely in the net. Would this be the 10-pounder? Nope, not quite. This one tipped the scales at just over 8 again, frustratingly.

Hang on — was I just disappointed by landing two 8 pound brown trout? Joining the double-figure club was starting to become an obsession . . .

Anthony's turn, and again he hooked up and landed another nice rainbow. As the rain started, we decided to keep the fish and head for cover. With a crackling open fire, enjoying a bottle (or two) of oaky chardonnay as our kōura muncher slowly cooked away, we recounted the day's many successes and near misses, while marvelling at the 'best in the world' country we live in. A place that still has plenty of secrets, especially if you know where to look and who to ask nicely.

> **Hang on, was I just disappointed by landing two 8 pound brown trout? Joining the double-figure club was starting to become an obsession . . .**

MAPLE MISO-MARINATED RAINBOW TROUT GRILLED ON CEDAR

ANTHONY MCNAMARA, LUXE
SERVES 4

Marinade

½ cup sake
¼ cup maple syrup
5 tablespoons white miso (shiro miso — be sure to use this rather than any of the darker, heavier misos)

1.5–3 kg rainbow trout fillets, skin-on

To serve

2 cups cooked sushi rice
ground sesame seeds, to season
powdered nori seaweed, to season
1 spring onion
1 bunch coriander
1 fresh chilli
200 g shredded tofu

Equipment

a board of untreated maple wood, or alternatively a split length of tōtara, mānuka or kānuka
half a dozen nails
a good-sized fire of mānuka wood, which has been allowed to burn down into white-hot coals

Marinade

Bring the sake to the boil in a small saucepan, and flame to burn off the alcohol, which might toughen the flesh of the fish. Add the maple syrup and miso and whisk until smooth.

Remove from the heat and allow to cool before using, or pouring into a jar and storing in the fridge.

To marinate the fish, brush a thick coating over the whole fillet and refrigerate for a few hours, or for up to three days. The longer the fish has been marinated for, the firmer the texture and the deeper the flavour.

Cooking

Put the marinated fillet skin-side down on the board and secure with a few lightly knocked-in nails around the edge.

Place the board at an angle next to your fire, close enough to cook the fish in the radiant heat, but not so close that the wood burns before the fish is cooked.

Keep a close eye on the fish, basting with marinade as it cooks, which should take 15–20 minutes. The fish is cooked when the flesh feels firm and cracks and yields slightly when pressed.

To serve

Serve with cooked sushi rice on the side, seasoned with ground sesame seeds, powdered nori seaweed, chopped spring onion, coriander and chilli, and shredded tofu.

10

FLOATING THROUGH FIJI

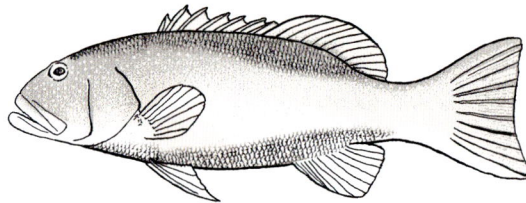

It's no secret that I like my trips into the Pacific to come with a little adventure — OK, a lot of adventure, with a touch of danger, and quite a bit of ocean. But getting the balance right between what you want from a holiday and what your partner wants can be tricky, especially when your 'hol-goals' are at the opposite ends of the relaxation spectrum. This is where the joy of untethering from land strikes what I think is a perfect balance, and Fiji is the perfect place to do this.

They say Fiji is where happiness finds you. Of all the Pacific Islands, it's the most visited tourist destination by far, greeting more than four times the visitors of its nearest rival each year. But it is what lies beyond the resorts of Denarau that holds the greatest attraction for me: an ocean of sparsely populated islands, of manta rays and sharks, and some of the best fishing the Pacific has to offer.

Those lucky enough to have escaped Denarau's safety net will know Fiji is actually an archipelago of a staggering 330 islands and over 500 islets. All are ringed by coral reefs, peppered across 18,000 sq km of azure blue

South Pacific ocean. What this means for sailors is calm, clear waters, safe anchorages and new views to wake up to every morning. There are stunning tropical Instagram clichés around every corner, each better than the last. But I'll get to that, because there is adventure to be had on the main islands as well.

Before I headed out into Fiji's wild blue yonder, I had a date with a jet boat and a reef alive with sharks. You can dive with sharks all over our planet, from the Arctic circle to southern New Zealand, but the Beqa Adventure Divers' shark dive is something else.

It's really three shark dives in one. To start, you head down 30 m to a place called 'The Arena'. There you are greeted by 40 or more 200 kg bull sharks — considered one of the most dangerous sharks on Earth. They are huge, and there is no cage to protect you. You simply hunker down behind a low coral wall while your Fijian guides feed them by dropping a constant flow of fish heads from a bin above, as well as by hand, as you watch just centimetres away. This is heart-in-your-mouth stuff — a dive I will never forget.

Then, on the way up, there's another feed at 'The Den', at around 15 m. This time it is grey reef sharks and the odd silvertip before you move up to your decompression stop at 5 m, which is thick with blacktip and whitetip reef sharks. It is something that simply has to be done to be believed.

Manoa Laivili of Beqa Adventure Divers says for every shark-diving guest, $25 dollars goes straight to the local village that traditionally owns the dive site. 'Now the villagers are more aware of protecting the whole ecosystem for their children's children to enjoy. The whole idea is to have sustainability not only for our present fish stocks, but looking ahead to the next generation as well.'

These experiences are great for the adventurous, but what about the partner who likes more of the comforts found on land? This is where the catamaran part of the trip comes in. Think of it as a floating boutique hotel rather than a boat, a hotel that can take you places. We hopped aboard Big Blue Fiji's 13.4 m sailing catamaran designed by

'Now the villagers are more aware of protecting the whole ecosystem for their children's children to enjoy. The whole idea is to have sustainability not only for our present fish stocks, but looking ahead to the next generation as well.'

— MANOA LAIVILI, BEQA ADVENTURE DIVERS

> **One of the things that attracts me most to the ocean is the lack of a defined path, the ability to pick your own destiny, to go where you want, when you want.**

French boatbuilders Lagoon specifically for charter sailing, to spend the next couple of days exploring just a few of Fiji's fabulous islands. These crewed boats come complete with four double cabins, each with their own en suite.

The beauty of a catamaran is its stability, the secret being its width — an incredible 7 m across. This, coupled with flat-water anchorages, means when the boat is at rest, even the most motion-sickness-prone will barely bat an eyelid or flutter a stomach. Unlike on a monohull, the shared space is elevated, allowing great views all around — perfect for when the sun slides into the sea at the end of the day and you're sitting at anchor. Piña colada, please.

One of the things that attracts me most to the ocean is the lack of a defined path, the ability to pick your own destiny, to go where you want, when you want. You get a real taste of this with bespoke catamaran cruising. Prior to leaving port, Captain Joe Donne and his partner, Laura, sat down and asked us what sort of things we wanted to see and do. They had no predetermined destination or specific out-of-the-box itinerary in mind — they simply wanted to go where we wanted to go. Obviously fishing and scuba diving were high on our agenda, but we could also have focused on surf breaks, deserted beaches, snorkelling, outer-island resort hopping, village visits, manta ray dives . . . or a combination of all of these and more.

Don't like the look of that island? Well, let's sail to the next. Dark clouds to the east? Let's go west. Fancy a wreck-dive? Joe knows just the spot, and as a qualified dive instructor he can sort that out as well. But the real beauty of being able to travel to your chosen activity means that when we wanted to go spearfishing, it was simply a case of going over the side of the boat. Anyone not interested simply stays aboard, perhaps

Previous spread
Malamala Beach Resort. A spectacular place to spend the day, especially when the food is prepared by chef Lance Seeto.

Opposite above
Say cheese! A 200 kg bull shark takes a fish head from the hand of one of the Beqa Adventure Divers guides.

Opposite below
The Arena is one of the world's best shark dives with upwards of 40 bull sharks feeding around the divers.

There, hiding under a ledge, was another nice coral trout, which, after carefully getting myself into position, I got with the spear.

lying on a beanbag suspended over the water in the hammock across the bows, enjoying a gentle ocean breeze and a good book, while being topped up with cool drinks by one of the crew. One party having gone off to get up to their necks in adventure, the other can blissfully zen-out in one of the most glorious locations on Earth.

For the first stage of our trip, we sailed from Denarau harbour to the famous surf island of Namotu. That evening we went out in the longboat, soft-bait rods in hand, attempting to catch coral trout. On every drop we caught fish and, after a variety of trevally and cod, I finally landed a spectacular orange-red coral trout — my target.

Next morning it was time to try my luck with the speargun. Diving along the same wall we had fished the night before, it was clear why we had hooked a fish every time. The reef was alive with some of the best numbers of fish I've seen in the Pacific. There, hiding under a ledge, was another nice coral trout, which, after carefully getting myself into position, I got with the spear.

Fish on ice, we then headed to Monuriki, where *Castaway* was filmed, then to the Sacred Islands, an island cluster known as the birthplace of Fiji. Here we spent a night at Navadra, going ashore to have a bonfire on a deserted beach before coming back to the Malamala Beach Club to deliver our fish to chef Lance Seeto, who prepared one of the most simple yet best fish dishes we had tasted in the islands, wai tom donu.

Leaving this trip, I knew I would never be able to look at a Fiji holiday in quite the same light again — not after having a taste of what the outer islands and a cruising catamaran can offer.

WAI TOM DONU (WATER, DIP, CORAL TROUT)

LANCE SEETO
SERVES 2

This is an ancient Fijian dish made with seawater. We used coral trout but any white-fleshed fish would work: snapper, tarakihi, butterfish, etc. This would be a perfect dish to make over a beach bonfire — very quick and simple.

1 whole (approx. 1–2 kg) scaled, gutted white-fleshed fish, with skin on

Dressing
½ red onion, diced
1 large tomato or several small tomatoes, flesh removed and diced
½ cup lime juice (or lemon juice)
1 cup clean seawater

To serve
½ cup freshly ground coconut flesh
½ pawpaw, julienned
handful edible flowers
juice of 1 kumquat (or lime or lemon)
coriander, to garnish

Score the skin of the fish on both sides, and place onto a hot barbecue or charcoal grill. The charcoaled skin of the fish is a key flavour, so don't be afraid to let it crisp and burn in parts.

Turn over as required.

While the fish is cooking, put the diced onion, tomato, lime juice and clean seawater into a shaker and give a good shake. Allow to sit and infuse while the fish cooks. The acid of the ingredients will offset the salty water.

To serve

Place the whole cooked fish onto a large plate with a lip. Liberally pour the infused dressing all over it.

Garnish the fish with fresh ground coconut, pawpaw, edible flowers and a squeeze of kumquat. Finish with coriander.

The dish is traditionally eaten with the fingers, so pinch some off and enjoy.

11

THE EIGHTH
WONDER

LOCATION
MILFORD SOUND, NEW ZEALAND

✕

FISH OF THE DAY
BLUE COD AND CRAYFISH

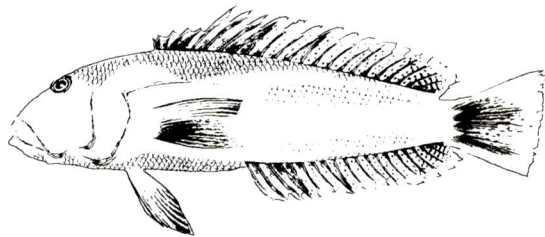

In the 1890s, author Rudyard Kipling described Milford Sound as the eighth wonder of the world. It's part of a World Heritage site, and has featured in box-office success stories like *The Lord of the Rings*. Everything is extreme here, from extreme weather to raging waterfalls, glacier-carved vertical mountains and deep, tannin-stained fiords teeming with life.

The Māori name for Milford Sound, Piopiotahi, means 'one single piopio' or the now extinct native thrush. One legend suggests this relates to the demigod Māui, who was killed by the goddess Hine-nui-te-pō. His pet piopio flew to the sound to mourn his death. Not much has changed here since Māui, or even Rudyard Kipling — certainly not the rainfall.

Visualise a blanket of water 7 m thick. Take the deep end of a swimming pool at about 2 m, and imagine three and a half of them stacked on top of each other. That's a huge volume of wet stuff, and it's the amount of average rainfall Fiordland experiences each year! Those 7 m of rainfall makes this one of the wettest places on Earth, but also arguably one of the most beautiful.

Previous spread
The view down the valley from the exit of the Homer Tunnel in Milford Sound.

Fresh water plays a pivotal part in this otherworldly pocket of New Zealand. It not only carved the mountains and valleys, providing postcard views at each bend of the fiord, but its sheer volume causes tannin-stained rivers and waterfalls to flow out on top of the salt water in the sound. This creates a surface layer that acts like a giant pair of sunglasses, in places 4 m or more thick. For divers this layer is surreal; where the fresh water mixes with the salt, it creates a trippy haze that can be quite disorientating. Below this is where the magic happens.

Having scuba and free-dived from the Three Kings off Cape Reinga to Stewart Island in the south, I can confidently say that nothing compares to this part of New Zealand's underwater. That tinted surface phenomenon produces an environment below in which light-sensitive organisms, usually found only at great depths, exist happily in the cool-water shallows. Here great fans of black coral, their white, waving arms hundreds of years old, create homes for sea dragons, brittle stars and mysterious nudibranchs.

Visualise a blanket of water 7 m thick. Take the deep end of a swimming pool at about 2 m, and imagine three and a half of them stacked on top of each other.

To witness tarakihi schooling along shorelines and hāpuku gathering beneath waterfalls is an experience worth the journey alone. Then there are the forests below. On the outer edges of the fiord, great tentacles of giant kelp wave in the swell and current, while inside the sound actual forests of trees washed out of the mountains and down rivers by that 7 m of annual rainfall literally blanket the sea floor. Through their ghostly forms, clouds of butterfly perch swim, while huge blue cod cruise on the periphery like mini submarines. And I haven't even mentioned the nests of crayfish.

In these dual layers of water exist two worlds. In the same location it's possible to see not only sea-run brown trout and fat salmon squirting past in the fresh top layer, but then a short duck dive later you can find yourself being appraised by a primitive sevengill shark in the salty

In these dual layers of water exist two worlds. It's possible to see not only sea-run brown trout and fat salmon squirting past in the fresh top layer, but a short duck dive later you can find yourself being appraised by a primitive sevengill shark in the salty darkness.

darkness. Surface again and you are looking at a near-vertical, snow-capped mountain range rising straight out of the sea just a few metres in front of you.

Those who are given a rare weather window to venture out of the fiords into open ocean off the untameable west coast are treated to a seascape that changes dramatically again. Above the water it comes alive with seabirds. Wing-tip water-touching mollymawk albatross, with their impeccable plumage, are made to look like mere pigeons in the presence of the largest of them all, the wandering albatross. Should you tire of their avian acrobatics then there's the bolshy Buller's albatross attempting to steal your catch next to the boat, or even little cape pigeons, a bird that appears much too delicate to exist in this at times brutal environment.

Send a line below and it's all about blue cod, hāpuku, tarakihi and spiny dogfish. Or, at the right time of year, runs of southern bluefin tuna are susceptible to a lure in just the right place. However, don't put anything shiny over the side here or you will find yourself suddenly competing with the South Island sailfish, otherwise known as the annoying and inedible New Zealand barracouta. These fanged silver slivers will scissor off all your gear not just in one place but often three or four, with not so much as a swivel or sinker spared by the determined marine marauders. Packs of them seem to hunt like wolves, and speaking of water wolves, it is not unusual to run into pods of orca off this coast too.

We were keen to get some blue cod and crayfish to cook up, so we stopped just inside the entrance to the sound, in 30 m of water only 5 m from the vertical rock wall of the fiord. Snorkelling down, I could see there was no shortage of crays, all of them out in the open, often in groups by small overhangs or cracks in the vertical face.

Opposite above
One of hundreds of crystal-clear rivers that flow through Fiordland National Park.

Opposite below
The hardest part of catching crayfish here is choosing which one to take, and how to avoid breaking the fragile black coral they are hiding beside.

TAMING the TROUT

TE ANAU

FIORDLAND · NEW ZEALAND

> **The problem I faced was twofold: which cray to grab, and how to get it without damaging the black coral trees they were clustered around in the process.**

The problem I faced was twofold: which cray to grab, and how to get it without damaging the black coral trees they were clustered around in the process — and I was only free-diving down about 15 to 20 m. It was incredible to see such an abundance of black coral so shallow.

With a few crayfish in the bin, we headed outside the fiord to chase some blue cod. Out in the open ocean we used our sounder to find some edges and reef structure around 20 to 40 m deep, then dropped baits down to the waiting cod below. Time after time the drop would end with barracouta taking the bait, the sinkers and even the swivels. Time and time again we would retie our gear, shift locations and try again. Eventually a lull in the sailfish allowed us to get a few blue cod to the boat — every one a monster. Then back in we went, before loading the trusty 4WD and slowly towing our boat up and out through the famous Homer Tunnel.

If you're keen to come dive and fish here, there are only a few options. You can tow your own boat in like we did, or you could join a trip with Pure Salt or Fiordland Charters. But for either of those two charter options expect a long wait to find a space — this place is popular, and for good reason.

Fiordland remains an essential Kiwi pilgrimage. Why? Because, of all the places in this great country of ours that we travelled to, no amount of column inches, photos or video will ever truly capture the majesty of this place. So if this year is the year you *finally* book a trip to come see for yourself, for goodness' sake, remember to take a raincoat and some industrial-grade insect repellent to ward off the hordes of hungry sandflies that attack any piece of exposed skin and photobomb every postcard picture.

Previous spread, clockwise from top left
One of the many things Milford Sound is known for — its stunning sunsets; The road in from Te Anau across the Eglinton River flats; With the chef's ingredients in hand, who can resist a photo op on the shores of Lake Te Anau; The kea can remove a car's chrome in just minutes with its tin-opener bill; As soon as you stop at the entrance to the Homer Tunnel, expect a visit from these cheeky parrots — the alpine kea.

Opposite above
The *Fish of the Day* Jeanneau sits in front of the Instagram-famous 151 m high Stirling Falls in Milford Sound.

Opposite below
Two solid Milford Sound red rock lobster or crayfish taken on snorkel.

PAN-SEARED BLUE COD, GARLIC RIBBON VEGETABLES, MASCARPONE AND HERB-CRUSHED POTATOES WITH BEURRE BLANC

RYAN (MUZZA) MURRAY
SERVES 2

Beurre blanc

50 ml white wine vinegar
150 ml white wine
1 bay leaf
4 peppercorns
300 ml cream
100–150 g butter, chilled
  and cubed

Main dish

6 medium potatoes
2 carrots
2 courgettes
2 fillets blue cod
150 g butter
small bunch chives, finely
  chopped
100 g mascarpone
oil
2 cloves garlic, finely diced
small bunch parsley, finely
  chopped

Beurre blanc

Place the vinegar, wine, bay leaf and peppercorns in a saucepan. Over a medium heat, reduce liquid by 75 per cent.

Remove the bay leaf and peppercorns. Put the pan back over the heat and add the cream. Reduce by 50 per cent. The reduced cream mix should be thick but not splitting.

Remove from the heat and whisk in the chilled butter, which will stop the reducing process. Whisk together well and set aside in a warm place until ready to use.

Main dish

Peel potatoes and boil until al dente. Wash the carrots and courgettes. Peel them into flat ribbons and set aside.

Remove the skin and any bones from the blue cod fillets. Cut each fillet into 2–3 pieces for ease of cooking. Be sure to pat the fillets dry with a paper towel to get a nice crust on the fish when cooking.

Once the potatoes are cooked, drain and add 100 g of butter, the chives and the mascarpone. Mix together with a spoon — not to mash but until well mixed/crushed.

Heat 2 large pans, to cook the fish and the ribbon veges. Heat a little oil in one pan and cook fish over a medium-high heat for a few minutes until a crust has formed on the outside. Add remaining butter. Turn to finish the other side — this should take only 2–3 minutes each side.

In the other pan, heat oil and quickly stir-fry the veges with garlic.

To serve

Load servings of spuds and vegetables onto each plate. Top with fish pieces, and finish with a good drizzle of beurre blanc sauce. Garnish with fresh parsley.

CRAYFISH KOKODA

SERVES 2

1 crayfish tail
1–2 limes
½ teaspoon flaky sea salt
¼ cup diced red onion
2 tablespoons chopped
  chives
6 cherry tomatoes, halved
2 pinches chilli flakes
¼–½ cup coconut cream
pepper to taste

Remove the crayfish flesh from the shell and dice into 1 cm cubes. Mix the lime juice well with the crayfish flesh and season with flaky sea salt. Set aside in the fridge for half an hour for the citrus acid to 'cook' the cray flesh.

After half an hour, remove the flesh from fridge and taste. It should have a nice balance between acid and salt, and be almost cooked through.

Add the onion, chives, cherry tomatoes and chilli, and mix well. Rest in fridge until ready to serve.

Before serving, add the coconut cream and season well.

12

THE WILD, WILD WEST

LOCATION
GOLDEN BAY TO JACKSON BAY,
WESTLAND, NEW ZEALAND

✕

FISH OF THE DAY
GEODUCK CLAMS

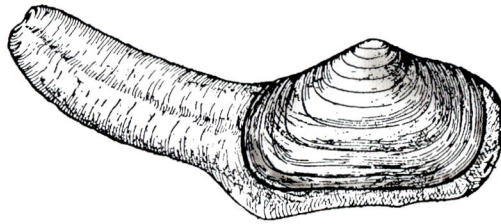

I t is home to one of the country's biggest national parks, and the waters that flow through it are some of the cleanest on Earth. Flowing from the mountains to the sea, this water is filtered by limestone in some of the deepest cave systems in the Southern Hemisphere. It is this same pure water that ensures some of the most productive shellfish beds you'll find anywhere remain intact. Welcome to Golden Bay, the starting point for our road trip down the West Coast of the South Island.

Today Tākaka, the Bay's largest town, is a multicultural success story, home to a rich tapestry of immigrants, largely from Europe, as well as an eclectic bunch of 'originals'. After a period of suspicion and sideways glances, 'hippies' and 'straights' now move freely amongst each other, the odd marriage benefiting from the different prism on life each brings to the table. Or so confess the local 'hippy' and self-confessed 'straight' sitting at my table after a bottle of the local finest has eased the conversation into a colourful and unique description of the area's rich history of convergence.

To paraphrase — and apologies for my recollection, but the wine was rather good — basically a whole lot of country folk, mostly farmers, were

Previous spread
Driving along State
Highway 6 on the wild
West Coast of the
South Island.

jolted from their idyllic sleepwalk through life when the New Zealand government, concerned about the flood of people leaving the regions for cities, opened up cheap plots of rural land in the 1970s. This coincided with a period of global consciousness, driven by a fear of nuclear war, coupled with a trend of being self-sufficient, that resulted in a bunch of newly minted hippies arriving en masse. What a small-town shock it must have been for the original Tākaka-dwellers when 400 polar-opposite new residents turned up in a single year, followed by even more the following year. The gently seasoned hippy very much enjoyed telling me of the initial hostility they faced, which resulted in a push-back from these newcomers that saw them get organised and eventually take over the local council.

I'm retelling you this because it goes a long way to explaining how this unique area has come to be. At the very least it explains why raw-milk gate sales are still legal here!

One of the typical locals we met was dairy farmer Sue Brown. Dairy often gets a bad rap for polluting New Zealand rivers and streams, and there are some bad eggs, but by and large dairy farmers today are working much harder to protect our waterways. Golden Bay locals have won an international award for the restoration of the Aorere River catchment, southwest of Collingwood, and Sue is proud of what she and her community have achieved.

Described as 'the champion of the valley', Sue has led the local farmers down a fringe-planting path that the whole of New Zealand can look to as an example of what can be done to improve the water quality of our streams and rivers. Today, five species of our native freshwater fish call this stream home — a huge achievement given how sensitive these species are to farm run-off.

'The farmers that live in the Aorere Valley all swim in the water, they all catch whitebait, they all go fishing in the coastal waters. So we all understood that there was an issue that we had to fix, and we did,' Sue explains. 'The big thing for us was understanding the land–water interface and what would work and what wouldn't work, as well as what was affordable.'

The West Coast is life in-your-face where tourists set out to remind themselves of their humanness, their blood and sinew, their free-thought and decision-making abilities — helped by a decided lack of cell-phone coverage.

As a community, the area's unique geography, complete with difficult access pinch-points, has allowed it to develop to be just a little bit different to the rest of New Zealand, and I like it a lot. This little piece of isolated New Zealand is a couple of hours' drive from Nelson, heading towards the South Island's northernmost sand sickle, via a hill the locals call Marble Mountain. This drive is an adventure in itself! The journey takes you from the Riwaka Resurgence, past the Ngārua Caves and the Te Waikoropupū (Pupū) Springs, with the clearest fresh water in the world, to the Anatoki salmon farm, where you can catch and eat your own fish within minutes of arriving.

Other attractions in the area include the family-run Farewell Spit Eco Tours, for some of the best bird-watching in the country, or walking the main drag of Tākaka for some of the best vegan food found anywhere. From the famous Mussel Inn to the fabulous Zatori Lodge, visitors are well catered to for entertainment, food and rest all wrapped up in a warm parcel aptly named Golden Bay.

But these other features were all just a happy bonus on top of what I had really come for. You see, another secret delicacy exists here that I can confidently say most New Zealanders have not a clue about, called geoduck but pronounced gooey-duck.

This rare breed of gaper shellfish exists in very few places in the world. The origin of their name is a clue to their appearance and title as the world's ugliest shellfish. It's derived from a Native American word that translates as 'burrowing genitals' — which brings me to their other moniker, 'penis clams'. Living to over 160 years of age and weighing up to 750 g each, they are considered a delicacy in Asia, where they can fetch upwards of $300 apiece. Your natural first thought upon seeing one is: which sicko figured out you could eat these? But I can now confirm that they taste like a cross between a scallop and an oyster. These surprisingly delicious shellfish are just another example of this special area of our country, where a bunch of unique inhabitants have been left to do their

Opposite above
A few of Golden Bay's sweet fat cockles, which were easily collected at low tide on the sand flats.

Opposite below
After 20 minutes of digging in the murky depths of Golden Bay, the prize — a geoduck clam.

own thing and develop in their own special way together.

To find our geoducks, we headed out off one of the Bay's beautiful golden-sand beaches to a depth of around 12 m. There we dived down on scuba looking for what local divers described as a pair of holes staring at you from the mud/sand substrate. What they didn't tell us was how hard that substrate was, and how deep these clams would be buried when you were trying to extract them. It took me almost 30 minutes to finally get a hold of my first one. Buried up to my shoulder and completely blinded by a cloud of murky sand and mud, I was absolutely ecstatic to finally drag it out of the sea floor. Now I see why professional geoduck divers use hydraulic pumps to blast them out! I was completely out of air by the time I had just three!

A few days in Golden Bay was a great start to our road trip, one that took us south down the West Coast as far as the road would take us. On paper, it might seem like an odd place to visit: steep, winding roads with few facilities; cold, wet weather; wild West Coast wind, wild West Coast beaches, wild West Coast locals and even wilder West Coast sandflies. Yet this is precisely what makes this stretch of the world so bloody great. It's no cruise on the Riviera, where the most dramatic thing you might do is spill prosecco on your chinos. The West Coast is life in-your-face where, in an increasingly homogenised world, tourists feel liberated enough to pick a path and set out to remind themselves of their humanness, their blood and sinew, their free-thought and decision-making abilities — helped by a decided lack of cell-phone coverage.

The further down the coast you drive, the more lumpy and warty it gets, in a good way. Jackson Bay was to be our final stop on this road trip to nowhere. This is a place most Kiwis would struggle to find on a map, yet it provides some of the only coastal shelter on the whole drive down. It's a gem of a spot, accentuated by a wharf running out at one end of the bay and a bright-orange converted railway carriage on the roadside dubbed The Cray Pot. Here exists a fish-and-chip recipe so protected that it was given to the new owners only under strict conditions that they must never share it. No amount of prying on my part could prise the secret batter ingredients from sisters Dana and Nicole. Alas, I had to leave empty-handed — but full of stomach.

SASHIMI GEODUCK

FRED ARCHER
SERVES 4

3 kawakawa leaves and
  3 dried kawakawa berries
½ lemon
3 geoducks
2 carrots
salt and ground white
  pepper
assortment of garnishes:
  sliced radish, broccolini
  florets, borage flowers,
  truffle oil

To cook the geoducks, place the kawakawa leaves, kawakawa berries and lemon into a pot of water and bring to the boil. Blanche the whole geoducks for 10–15 seconds only, depending on size, then lift out with a slotted spoon. Keep the liquid for use as chowder stock (see opposite page).

To prepare the geoducks, remove the shell. Peel the outside skin layer from the main syphon, then separate the meat into the three main components — syphon, main muscle and mantle, cleaning off any sand or silt as you work. Slice the syphon very thinly for the sashimi element, and retain the meatier parts of the clam for the chowder.

Peel and finely slice the carrots. Boil them in a small pot, just covered in water, until soft. Modestly season with salt and ground white pepper, then purée.

Place a dollop of purée on each plate, and arrange sashimi beautifully on top and garnish to your taste.

GEODUCK CHOWDER

Spice paste

1 stalk lemongrass, roughly chopped
2 kaffir lime leaves
2 cloves garlic
1 chilli, seeds included or not, depending on preference
30 mm chunk of galangal, peeled
30 mm ginger root, peeled
zest of 1 lime
small bunch coriander
splash of coconut cream, to blend (open a tin and save the rest)

Chowder

24 cockles
1 cup white wine
geoduck stock (from recipe on opposite page)
1 onion, diced
1 carrot, diced
2 stalks celery, diced
olive oil
salt
30 g butter
25 g flour
8 urenika potatoes, cooked in the geoduck stock from recipe on opposite page
fillets from 2 or 3 medium white fish (blue cod, gurnard or snapper), roughly chopped,
meat picked from the fish heads and frames, cooked in the geoduck stock from recipe on opposite page
meat from 3 geoducks, reserved from recipe on opposite page
juice of ½ lemon
black pepper
coriander, chopped
buttered white bread, to serve

Spice paste

Mix all of the ingredients in a food processor, until a paste consistency. Add a little more coconut cream if needed.

Chowder

Cover the cockles in white wine and quickly cook. Shell them, reserving the meat. Add the cooking liquid to the geoduck stock (from Sashimi Geoduck recipe on opposite page).

In a heavy-bottomed pot, over a medium heat, cook off the onion, carrot and celery in a good splash of olive oil with a pinch of salt.

After 2 minutes add the blended spice paste, and cook for a further 3 minutes. Add the butter and, once that has melted, the flour. This will form a roux, or the base for thickening the sauce. The consistency should be sticky, but not too dry.

Start pouring in the geoduck stock, a cup at a time, stirring constantly as the chowder begins to thicken. Once the soup base has the desired consistency, add the potatoes, fish fillets and picked meat, geoduck meat and cockle meat. Cook gently for a few minutes until the white fish has just cooked through.

Finally, squeeze in half a lemon, season generously with black pepper and adjust the salt if necessary (although with the saltiness of the shellfish, not much additional salt should be needed).

Serve with a sprinkling of chopped coriander and large chunks of warm, buttered white bread.

13

FAST FISH

LOCATION
RAROTONGA

✕

FISH OF THE DAY
WAHOO

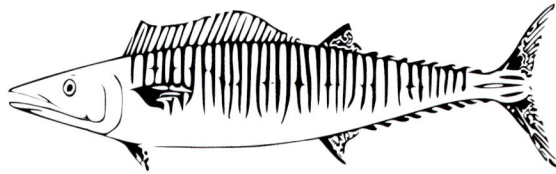

Rarotonga is an extinct volcano rising from the sea floor 4000 m below to form a tiny island just 9 km long and 6 km across. It is an oasis in a sea of blue, attracting every ocean wanderer for miles and miles.

Just a four-hour hop from Auckland, Raro is one of New Zealand's favourite holiday destinations. The flight might be quick, but the wormhole you travel through on the way there changes everything. It is as if time simply slows down. Queuing in the tropical heat to clear customs, all those city woes you've just left behind sink into the abyss as the anticipation of what adventures lie ahead bubbles up to fill the void.

For keen spearos like myself, Rarotonga offers some serious blue-water challenges. I was here chasing one such challenge: the wahoo, considered one of the fastest-accelerating fish in the ocean. I wanted to get one on rod and another one on spear, but shooting a fish that can weigh up to 80 kg and is capable of speeds in excess of 70 kph requires good kit and a steely nerve. And did I mention their razor-sharp teeth?

Getting one on the rod was to be the first mission, but to do that we needed maroro or flying fish for bait — and for the barbecue too.

If you have been to Rarotonga, or even Tahiti, you may have seen the weird-looking boats in the marinas — wooden-hulled mahimahi boats. The driver sits perched in a hole up on the bow, where the anchor locker would be on most boats. Yeah, crazy, I know, but there's more. There is no steering wheel, just a vertical wooden post in front of the driver that he throws left or right to steer. They use these boats to chase down and harpoon mahimahi by day, but at night they take on another life, that of the maroro hunter. Harpoons are swapped for long-handled nets, and the drivers wear crash helmets with a powerful spotlight bolted to the front, wired to the boat's battery. Why the helmet? Maroro often fly straight at the light, so getting smacked in the head by one is a common occurrence.

These crazy night-hunters race across the blackness, swerving and turning at speed, chasing down these crazy little fish. Spooked by the spotlight, they take to the air, and the chase begins. As they land, the net comes down, scooping them up and depositing them in the back of the boat with a flick of the wrist.

That's if the driver is fast enough, because there is another hunter on the prowl. Giant trevally have learned the ways of the maroro hunters and bow-ride the boats, looking for an easy meal in the pool of the spotlight.

It is a real Raro experience so, if you're keen, find a fisherman to take you out — you won't be disappointed. Oh, and make sure he puts a few on the barbecue afterwards — they are absolutely delicious. No wonder they're the best tow-baits for wahoo . . . and mahimahi, and yellowfin, and marlin . . . actually, for anything.

Next morning, with a chilly bin of fresh maroro, we joined Akura Fishing Charters. And, while there are a lot of great charter operators in Raro to head out with, we had never missed with Akura on past trips, catching plenty of yellowfin and mahimahi. They were confident they could get us our wahoo without too much trouble.

We had a pair of maroro we had caught the night before, carefully stitched into nose weights, running long behind the boat. On the short

corners we were running small skirted lures, and towing the lot at around 8 knots.

Suddenly, one of the reels started screaming: a tell-tale wahoo strike. They go hard and fast, but rarely have much energy left after that first scorching run. Sure enough, after one and a half runs we got a solid 15 kg wahoo to the boat. Once it was gaffed and then hauled into the boat, we could get a better look at — and avoid — the fish's razor jaws. The best way to describe them is being like a set of diamond-sharpened pinking shears. Don't get bitten!

Wahoo go hard and fast, but rarely have much energy left after that first run. Sure enough, after one and a half runs we got a solid 15 kg fish to the boat.

With the first part of my goal achieved, now I wanted to land one on spear. Easier said than done, however! After two days diving every FAD (fish aggregation device) around the island we still had no wahoo. It was time to take a break and regroup.

I'd heard about another cool opportunity up here: there's a 'whale lady' and a whale research centre. Why? Well, Rarotonga is also a hotspot for migrating humpbacks, and you can see them off the beach most days from July to September. You can't swim with them here like you can in Niue, Tonga or Tahiti, but you can get out on a boat to see them or even spend time with 'whale lady' Nan Hauser and her research team.

Nan has been studying whales up here for close to 30 years. If you want to know about population abundance, acoustics, genetics, behaviour, migration or how these leviathans navigate, just ask Nan. She will boil over with the exuberant enthusiasm of a highly knowledgeable five-year-old. She is a trustee of the Save Our Oceans Charitable Trust in Rarotonga, and played a role in the creation of the Cook Islands' 2 million sq km whale sanctuary.

She says one of her favourite things about the whales is hearing their songs.

'Only the males sing, and every year their song changes and every whale in the area learns the new song. If you go to other parts of the world the song is different too. They can also make sounds that sound

Opposite above
A mother humpback whale and her calf just offshore from Muri Lagoon in Rarotonga.

Opposite below
The crown of thorns starfish, well known for its ability to consume large areas of fast-growing corals in the Pacific.

like cows and elephants — it's the funniest thing to have a forty-five-thousand-pound animal going moo.'

Now, back to the wahoo. One of the things that has always made *Fish of the Day* a difficult show to film is our targeting of a specific species each episode. Most of us can go to sea to catch fish and almost always come home with a feed. But it's incredible how when you want one particular type of fish, they all simply disappear — especially when the camera comes out.

Our adrenaline-fuelled elation must have been heard by every boat within a kilometre when I got hold of my fish.

Trying to catch a wahoo on spear was proving no different. Back out on the water, we had just one more morning to try to get one. I slipped into the water at FAD after FAD to no avail. Finally, with the crew shouting at me to return to the boat, a solid fish swam up from the depths to within range . . . or was it? The hardest thing about spearing in the tropics in crystal-clear water is trying to figure out just how far away the fish is from you, and I've had plenty of shots fall short. Often the fish is bigger than I thought and much further away.

This time I waited another couple of beats of that razor tail before pulling the trigger. It all happened so quickly. The next second I found myself getting towed at warp speed across the ocean, as my wahoo accelerated away from me and into the blue.

As I mentioned above, luckily they are usually a one-run wonder, so all that was required was for my spear to stay in the fish and my floats and the stretch in my line to soak up the blistering speed. And so it came to pass. Our adrenaline-fuelled elation must have been heard by every boat within a kilometre when I got hold of my fish. Dragging it on board I realised just how big it was: 1.7 m long and close to 30 kg. That fish remains the biggest wahoo I've ever shot.

We have a routine that we film at the end of each show, where I carry my fish through town to be prepared by the chef, often through quite crowded locations. I have to say I got plenty of strange looks, cheers and car-horn beeps from locals as I wandered about, heavy fish draped across my shoulders.

Previous spread, clockwise from top left
Whale researcher Nan Hauser and I laughing at the weird sounds made by male humpback whales singing under the boat; Mother and calf humpback swimming through the clear Rarotonga water; Maroro on the barbecue, these are spectacular eating fish; Two solid wahoo caught using whole flying fish baits; Walking my wahoo to the Nautilus Resort to meet up with chef Michael Fosbender; Proudly holding my personal best wahoo, speared in Rarotonga.

PAN-FRIED WAHOO WITH PRAWN AND CHILLI SALSA AND VANILLA COCONUT SAUCE

MIKE FOSBENDER
SERVES 4

Poached prawns

2 bay leaves
2 teaspoons whole black peppercorns
1 tablespoon citrus peel
1 tablespoon salt
600 g prawn cutlets

Prawn and pawpaw salsa

2 hot red chillies
600 g poached prawns (from above recipe), cut into bite-sized pieces
2 spring onions, white only, finely sliced
4 teaspoons Rito virgin coconut and chilli oil (or other quality virgin coconut oil and chilli oil mixed to taste)
juice of 1 lime
salt and pepper
1 pawpaw, peeled and diced
1 avocado, diced
handful coriander sprigs
virgin avocado oil

Vanilla coconut sauce

2 vanilla beans, split and scraped
2 cups dark rum
2 stalks lemongrass, chopped
1 litre coconut cream (Kara if possible)
100 ml coconut water
1 teaspoon lime juice
salt and white pepper to taste

Wahoo

1.5 kg fresh wahoo fillet
splash of cooking oil
sea salt
juice of 2 limes

Poached prawns

Bring half a pot of water to the boil. Add all ingredients except prawns, simmer for 1 minute then throw in the prawns and turn the heat off immediately. Let it sit for 3 minutes then strain the prawns and plunge into ice water to cool.

Prawn and pawpaw salsa

Cut the chillies lengthways, scrape out the seeds and cut into thin slices. Mix with the rest of the ingredients except the pawpaw, avocado, coriander and avocado oil. Adjust the seasoning.

When ready to serve, add the pawpaw, avocado and coriander, then finish with some virgin avocado oil.

Vanilla coconut sauce

Place the vanilla, rum and lemongrass in a pot and reduce until almost no liquid remains. Add the coconut cream and allow to simmer for 5–10 minutes over a low heat. The sauce should now be thick and rich, so thin down with the fresh coconut water.

Season with the lime juice, salt and white pepper, then strain into a clean pot. Bring back to a simmer before use.

Wahoo

Preheat oven to 180°C. Cut the wahoo into eight even-sized pieces, across the fillet. Turn each portion on its side and cut down the middle of the fillet, parallel to the skin.

Warm an ovenproof frying pan over medium heat and add oil. Rub some salt on the skin of each of the pieces of wahoo, then place in the pan, skin-side down. Repeat with the other pieces of wahoo, without the skin. Lightly season the top side of the fish while still in the pan. Allow to cook until golden, then flip over and take off the heat.

Squeeze over the lime juice and place in oven for 3–5 minutes. When cooked, the flesh of the fish should spring back firmly when pushed.

To serve

Pile a good amount of prawn salsa onto each warmed plate. Top with fish and drizzle with vanilla coconut sauce.

14

THE HAURAKI

LOCATION
HAURAKI GULF, NEW ZEALAND

✕

FISH OF THE DAY
KINGFISH AND GURNARD

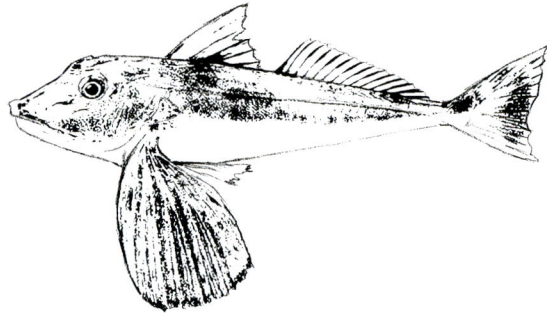

Every summer, the largest influx of tourists to New Zealand all arrive by sea, and go largely unnoticed. I'm not talking about the bum-bag-wearing cruise-ship wanderers of Wynyard Quarter, or the fancy-set sailors who arrive via super yacht. No, I'm talking about the visiting pelagic fish species that arrive on the warm-current conveyor belt from the tropics that pushes down from the north. All aboard for an Aotearoa summer, no passports required.

They arrive in their millions, all attracted by the bounty of baitfish and plankton that our warming summer waters overflow with. I often wonder, if more people could see the tropical paradise that exists on our doorstep, would it create a stronger connection between us and the sea?

On one trip out wide to blue water we ventured beyond the Hauraki Gulf to the east of Great Barrier Island. In just one day, a stone's throw from our country's most populous city, we managed to see an incredible array of visitors: two marlin, a short-billed spearfish, mahimahi, schools of skipjack tuna, swarms of saury (a tropical baitfish), a pod of large whales, two manta rays, one spine-tailed devil ray, and over 50 sunfish or mola mola. When we

Previous spread
Casting soft baits to a huge school of trevally and kahawai off the Mokohinau Islands in the Hauraki Gulf.

got back to shore I also learned that someone in the nearby Coromandel had landed a wahoo, and that a whale shark had also been seen.

A friend asked if I had gone all the way to Indonesia or somewhere else in the tropics to see all these things, unaware that they are all here, much closer to home. He was surprised when I told him that the manta ray was at Channel Island, a small island just inside the Hauraki Gulf off the tip of the Coromandel. People are also surprised to learn that the gulf itself is home to approximately 40 resident baleen whales called Bryde's whales (pronounced 'brooders'). Sealife Kelly Tarlton's aquarium also runs a rehab programme for exhausted turtles that turn up off northern shores — not that some have had to travel far, with several estuaries in the Far North boasting small numbers of year-round inhabitants. Some turtles enjoy their stay at Kelly Tarlton's so much that no matter where they are released, they swim right back to the aquarium and attempt to get back in! It's hard to beat good food, especially when it's free.

Some turtles enjoy their stay at Kelly Tarlton's so much that no matter where they are released, they swim right back to the aquarium and attempt to get back in! It's hard to beat good food, especially when it's free.

Another summer visitor we used to get in great numbers is the yellowfin tuna. However, due to commercial exploitation in offshore waters, visits from these magnificent yellow-sickled beasts are now rare. Whereas once, in season, you could catch them just a few hundred metres off Castle Rock near Hot Water Beach on the Coromandel, they now are so scarce that a fishing tournament in honour of them in Whakatane was forced to change its name. A few do still sneak through each year, and numbers have been rebuilding, but they are still just a tiny fraction of what this fishery used to be.

A major cause of this decline happened a few years back, when super-seiners using satellite telemetry located their tropical spawning grounds and pursed yellowfin to the point of collapse. If nothing else it proves that fish aren't bound by borders, and going forward we are all going to have to better manage all fisheries, as demand increases.

'Of all the types of seabirds in the
world, over 20 per cent — 70 different
species — can be found in the geographical
armpit of the North Island. Among them
are five types of seabirds that breed
nowhere else in the world.'

— CLARKE GAYFORD

As recreational fishers, I believe we have an obligation to conserve and protect our environment. After all, if we want to catch fish in the future, we have to ensure that we stand up and be counted when it comes to protecting these valuable assets. Whether you're in Asia, the Pacific or New Zealand, the end game is the same: look after our fish, look after our coastal ecosystems, and the generations to come might just be lucky enough to see, catch and eat tomorrow what we do today.

So back to the gulf . . . inside its boundaries there are more than 50 islands. Who knew? And it holds one of the most astounding concentrations of life found just about anywhere on Earth. Our little gulf contains a staggering 20 per cent of the world's biodiversity of seabirds. Let that hang in an updraft for a second. Of all the types of seabirds in the world, over 20 per cent — 70 different species — can be found in the geographical armpit of the North Island. Among them are five types of seabirds that breed nowhere else in the world. All of this is why the race to arrest the current degradation of the gulf's waters, caused by the pressures of nearby urbanisation, farming run-off and overfishing, is so important.

Slow fishing days have turned me into a bit of a bird-nerd, to help pass the time. Knowing which birds are which also helps with fishing, as certain birds will hover over certain types of baitfish, improving your chances of catching what swims underneath if you can identify them correctly.

The gulf's many islands hold some rare treasures, too. Anyone who has tried to book a stay on Tiritiri Matangi, a protected reserve island off the tip of the Whangaparāoa Peninsula, will tell you how popular that destination has become — it's often booked months in advance.

Another nearby island that is not so visitor-friendly is often described as the jewel in the Department of Conservation's (DOC's) crown. There is no landing allowed and almost no visitor access for good reason. Te Hauturu-o-Toi or Little Barrier Island has been a reserve since 1896, and is completely predator-free, thanks to a mammoth trapping and pest eradication programme. Our largest wētā and the stitchbird or hihi were once common on mainland New Zealand, but were all but wiped out by introduced pests. They now exist in the world only thanks to pest-free island oases like Hauturu. To hear the birdsong on the island is to step back in time, and get a glimpse of how amazing a predator-free environment could be.

Previous spread
The clear waters of the Mokohinau Islands looking south to Te Hauturu-o-Toi or Little Barrier Island.

Opposite above
With Department of Conservation's Nicola Toki and a couple of our largest insect — the giant wētā — on Te Hauturu-o-Toi.

Opposite below
Holding a young tuatara on Te Hauturu-o-Toi.

'Knowing which birds are which also helps with fishing, as certain birds will hover over certain types of baitfish, improving your chances of catching what swims underneath if you can identify them correctly.'

— CLARKE GAYFORD

Nicola Toki, DOC's first threatened species ambassador, who we met on Hauturu, says she wishes she could bring every New Zealander there 'and just plonk them in the bush . . . so they can just listen. This is what our forest is supposed to sound like.

'The reason for silent forests is simply because predators have come in and wiped out all the native birds. We know what the recipe is. The recipe is really simple. Take away the predators and maintain the habitat.'

With limited resources, not enough people and nowhere near enough funding, the DOC team battles on. Places like Hauturu are a testament to that dedication to saving our vulnerable native flora and fauna. I'm glad our environmental identity remains unique, and that people care enough to try to save it.

We have shot four episodes of *Fish of the Day* in the Hauraki Gulf over the past few years, targeting kahawai, snapper, kingfish and gurnard. For our first episode here we fished around Waiheke and Channel Island, between Great Barrier Island and the Coromandel, chasing kahawai on fly as well as with spear.

Kahawai are underrated, as both a fighting fish and a table fish — gone are the days of smoking them or just keeping them for bait. We even recently aged one for 10 days before consuming it raw, and I have to say it was the best sashimi (other than bluefin) that I had had in a long time.

For kingfish, we headed to the Mokohinau Islands, one of my favourite Hauraki Gulf fishing spots. It's not often you miss out there, and the kingfish can be big. On one trip with my producer Mike we both landed fish over 30 kg with the speargun. We also did a show specifically targeting gurnard: who knew you could fish specifically for them rather than just hooking a few while snapper fishing?

And it's the snapper fishing that the Hauraki Gulf is renowned for. New Zealand's largest concentration of recreational fishers exist here almost solely because of the snapper fishery. They are revered as one of our top table fish, and every summer they move in as the waters warm, congregating in schools to wait for the water to hit the magical 18°C mark. This is the temperature that triggers their annual spawning event on mass.

Whether it is a picnic on Motuihe, a ferry ride to Rangitoto or a visit with the takahē of Tiri, such is the range of activities available in the gulf that there really is something for everyone. All you need to do is get out there and enjoy.

Previous spread, left
Loading my speargun next to the boat off the coast of Te Hauturu-o-Toi.

Previous spread, right
A solid kingfish for chef Peter Gordon.

KINGFISH TOFU CURRY

PETER GORDON
SERVES 4

Coconut yoghurt
1 cup strained yoghurt
¼ cup fresh grated coconut (or use lightly toasted desiccated coconut if easier)
½ teaspoon lime zest
2 tablespoons shredded coriander leaves and stalks
1 teaspoon wasabi paste (optional)
sea salt

Freekeh salad
250 g freekeh
1 tablespoon olive oil
1 shallot, thinly sliced
pinch chilli powder
1 teaspoon smoked seaweed granules

Curry
1 tablespoon oil
2 shallots, thinly sliced
2 cloves garlic, thinly sliced
1 tablespoon sliced ginger
1 green chilli, diced
400 ml coconut cream
1 x 10 cm stick of lemongrass, thinly sliced (discard the outer 2 layers and the bottom 1 cm — it's too woody)
4 coriander roots, washed and finely chopped
1 tablespoon tamarind paste
300 g silken tofu, cut into 2 cm cubes
500 g fresh kingfish cut into pieces around 2–3 cm square

Coconut yoghurt
Mix everything together and season with sea salt to taste.

Freekeh salad
Rinse the freekeh briefly in a sieve and leave to drain. Heat a medium-sized pan over medium-high heat and add the olive oil.

Add the shallot and cook until caramelised, stirring often. Stir in the chilli powder and seaweed.

Pour in the freekeh and 500 ml water, bring to the boil, then put the lid on and lower the heat to a simmer.

Cook until the freekeh is almost cooked but still a little al dente — about 10–12 minutes.

Turn off the heat and leave to cool with the lid on, unless you want to eat it hot.

Curry
Heat the oil in a large saucepan. Once hot, add the shallots, garlic and ginger and cook until golden, stirring often. Add the chilli and fry until the shallots are caramelised.

Add the coconut cream, lemongrass, coriander and tamarind and bring to a simmer. Add the tofu and cook for 2 minutes.

Add the kingfish and gently mix everything together. Cook for 3–5 minutes, until the fish is cooked but the middle is a little bit raw.

To serve
Serve curry on freekeh salad with a generous serve of coconut yoghurt on top.

SEARED GURNARD WITH SCALLOP AND SALSA CEVICHE

PETER GORDON
SERVES 2

1 large gurnard (approx. 1–1.5 kg), filleted and pin-boned — keep the skin on
cooking oil
4–6 scallops, depending on size
½ avocado, diced
2 asparagus — peel the base then thinly slice the whole thing
2 small kawakawa leaves (or use 8 basil leaves)
4 Vietnamese mint leaves (or use 10 regular mint leaves)
2 cm lemongrass stem, thinly sliced (from the softer inside — avoid the fibrous outer leaves)
½ red chilli, finely chopped (more or less to taste)
½ teaspoon lemon zest
juice of 1–2 lemons
sea salt

To serve

½ sweet, crunchy apple, julienned
½ teaspoon chilli oil (I used one made by an Auckland producer called Banu's, which also contained peanuts and sesame seeds)
zest and juice of 1 lime, or zest and juice of ½ lemon
flaky sea salt

Season the gurnard fillets and lightly oil them. Remove the roe from the scallops and dice it. Slice each scallop in half, to give you two circles.

Add the scallop roe to the avocado, asparagus, kawakawa, Vietnamese mint, lemongrass and chilli. Gently mix together, then mix in the lemon zest and juice and a little sea salt.

Heat a heavy-based pan over medium-high heat. Lay the gurnard fillets in, skin-side down, and cook for 2 minutes (less for smaller fish). Turn over and cook to caramelise the white flesh.

To serve

Place some raw scallop meat on each plate, lay some apple julienne on top and place some fish on top of the apple. Spoon over the scallop roe salsa and drizzle with chilli oil. Grate some lime or lemon zest on top, squeeze with lime or lemon juice and sprinkle with a little flaky sea salt.

KAHAWAI TACOS

ANTHONY MCNAMARA, LUXE
SERVES 4

Salsa

1 tablespoon olive oil
3–4 cloves garlic, whole
   and unpeeled
1 large green chilli
1 green tomato
handful coriander, stems
   and leaves separated
sea salt
juice of 1 ripe lime
2–3 spring onions, finely
   shredded

Kahawai

4 tablespoons plain flour
1 egg, lightly beaten
1 packet plain corn tortilla
   chips, smashed into
   crumbs
skinned and boned fillets
   from one large kahawai
   (approx. 2–3 kg), cut into
   finger-sized pieces

To serve

8 soft corn tortillas or
   tacos (the Tio Pablo
   brand is very good if you
   do not wish to make your
   own)
butter, for frying
sea salt
1 ripe avocado, smashed to
   a rough guacamole with
   the juice of 1 lime
half an iceberg lettuce,
   very finely shredded

Salsa

You'll want to make the salsa first, to give it a little time for the full flavour to develop. In a small pan or skillet, heat a tablespoon of olive oil and add the garlic, chilli and the whole green tomato, turning to coat everything evenly in the oil before roasting in a medium oven until everything is browned and slightly softened. This will take about 10–15 minutes. (This stage could also be done on a barbecue — the desired end result is for the tomato to have a charred skin and softened flesh.)

Allow everything to cool, and then peel the skins from the garlic and the chilli. Cut the green tomato into wedges and set aside until serving.

In a mortar and pestle (or small food processor), grind the coriander stems, peeled garlic and chilli with a little sea salt, until you have a thick, green, aromatic paste. Add the lime juice, spring onions and coriander leaves and mix well, without losing any of the texture of what you have just added.

Kahawai

To crumb the fish, set out three bowls: one containing the flour, one the beaten egg and one the tortilla crumbs.

Pass the pieces of fish through these in that order, making sure that each coating is even but not excessive. The flour will stick to the fish, the egg to the flour and the crumb to the egg.

Put the crumbed fish pieces back into the refrigerator for half an hour, or overnight, to chill, firm up and to allow the crumb coating to set before cooking.

To serve

Wrap the soft corn tortillas in foil and place in a medium-low oven to warm through. They will only need a couple of minutes, while the fish cooks.

Recipe continued over page . . .

Heat a skillet with a little sizzling butter, and cook the kahawai pieces until golden brown and crispy all over. Season the fish with a little sea salt after it has been cooked.

Take the warm corn tortillas from the oven, spread with a spoonful of guacamole, add a piece of fish, some roast green tomato, a spoonful of salsa, and then some finely shredded lettuce.

Enjoy two tacos as an entrée or four as a generous main course, with extra limes and ice-cold cervezas on the side.

COCONUT SNAPPER CEVICHE

MARK SOUTHON
SERVES 4

400 g snapper fillets, skinned and boned
juice of 2–3 limes
1–2 kaffir lime leaves, very finely chopped
sea salt
1 spring onion, finely sliced
½ red chilli, thinly sliced
coriander and mint to taste, finely chopped
1 tomato, diced
¼ cucumber, diced
100 ml coconut cream
½ rock melon, peeled, seeded and diced

Thinly slice the snapper and place in a large bowl. Add the lime juice and leaves and a sprinkle of sea salt, then leave to marinate for five minutes.

Add the spring onions, chilli, herbs, tomato and cucumber and stir through. There should be a good balance of ingredients and colours in the bowl.

Stir through the coconut cream. Check the seasoning, adding a little more sea salt and lime if needed, then arrange in serving bowls. Sprinkle over some melon and serve.

PAN-FRIED SNAPPER WITH A SMOKED TOMATO BUTTER SAUCE

MARK SOUTHON
SERVES 4

Sauce

1 kg tomatoes
salt
6–8 basil leaves
splash of cream
50 g Whitestone smoked
   mānuka butter or flavour
   regular butter with smoke
   flavour
juice of ½ lemon
fresh basil leaves, chopped

Fish

4 good-sized snapper
   fillets (180 g each), skin
   on
cooking oil
60 g prawns, diced
50 g chorizo, diced
60 g sweet corn kernels
4 tablespoons of sweet
   corn purée
1 teaspoon spring onion oil

Sauce

Roughly chop the tomatoes, and place in a food processor with a good pinch of salt and the basil leaves. Pulse 5–6 times, then hang overnight in a sieve lined with a coffee filter to strain out liquid. Heat this liquid in a pot to reduce it by half, add a small splash of cream and whisk in enough butter to thicken.

Season, then finish the sauce with a little squeeze of lemon and freshly chopped basil.

Fish

Dry the skin of the snapper. Add a little oil to a medium-hot pan and cook the fish skin-side down for 5–6 minutes, or until the skin is golden and crispy. Flatten the fillet slightly to ensure a level surface and even colouring.

Flip the fish and cook for 1 minute then remove from the pan and keep warm. To the same pan, add the prawns and chorizo and sauté for 1 minute, then add the corn kernels and warm through.

To serve

Swipe some warmed corn purée onto each plate, spoon over the prawn and chorizo mix and top with some fish, then drizzle over some sauce and spring onion oil.

15

SAMOA SOJOURN

LOCATION
SAMOA

FISH OF THE DAY
YELLOWFIN TUNA

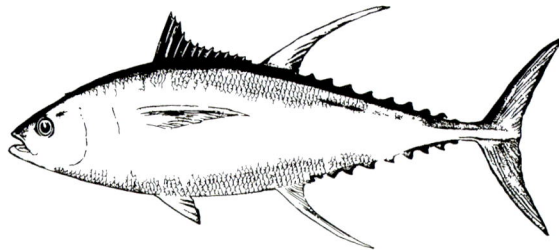

I've been lucky enough to go to Samoa more than half a dozen times for work and play, including a glorious month and a half once doing some voluntary work. There are around 25,000 islands in the Pacific. All are extraordinary in their own right, with different languages, cultures, geography, climate and, of course, fish. But Samoa has a real feeling of home to it — the cleanliness, the laughter and the real sense of family you get from all the wonderful people you meet.

It's always great when a place you've been to previously and thought you knew suddenly presents itself in a way that changes your whole outlook. To me Samoa has always been a place that ticks all the boxes of the things I want from a tropical getaway. It's connected enough with its local culture to feel like you are somewhere else, but still has enough of the comforts of home so that nothing is a stress.

Sure, you can stay in one of the nicer resorts on offer — there are plenty to choose from — but it also caters to the budget-conscious and adventurous. One of my favourite escapes was on the quiet side of the island Upolu, staying in a village fale on the water's edge. It was

Previous spread
The spectacular and very affordable Matareva Beach fales on the south shore of Upolu Island, Samoa.

basically a single-room hut on an elevated platform equipped with just a mattress and a mosquito net. At night a pack of local dogs slept underneath it, howling at the moon so loudly that I recorded them and set it as my ringtone. That cost me just 70 tālā (around 39 NZ dollars) a day including breakfast and dinner, while also providing a proper village experience.

That trip also happened to coincide with the annual palolo worm harvest. Once a year, on a full moon, these reef-dwelling marine worms, about 40 cm long, break in half, with their reproductive tails swimming to the surface to release their eggs and milt (semen) as a swarm of locals with nets and headlamps descend on them. Perhaps this is not everyone's idea of a good time, but for me I was like a pig in the proverbial. (Pig was on the menu, too.) Combine all of that with an accessible surf break right in front of my hut and this was one of the more memorable holidays I've ever had.

Having had all such experiences, I thought I knew the island and its surrounding reefs fairly well. The permanent scar on my back from a surf accident means that they certainly know me intimately! So to be honest when it came to fishing I made assumptions based on having never heard anyone say boo about the place's fishing potential. I quite wrongly assumed that the local reefs must be depleted, and the islands' waters contained only a few passing pelagics.

It's difficult to describe how good it felt to be so wrong about this. It's even harder to describe just how good we struck the fishing there. We went to film just one episode, which quickly became two, something we've done only a few times during all our shoots.

Our guide to the local delights on this trip was Greg 'Hoppo' Hopping from Troppo Fishing Adventures, possibly the most Australian man I've ever met. He's the type of bloke who could have easily played an uncle in the movie *The Castle* — perhaps an uncle that had shot through, Blue, escaping the flaming rat race to wind up in the tropics, a few skeletons neatly tucked away. Probably. I liked him instantly.

Following spread
Find the schools of bluefish here in Samoa and you find the predator fish like Spanish mackerel and giant trevally.

'Seventy-five metres in front of us. See the shimmy? One o'clock. *One o'clock!* Come on, get it together, you're chilling out. I'm not chilling out. I'm excited! It won't matter what you throw in the water, they're gunna grab it!'

— GREG 'HOPPO' HOPPING, TROPPO FISHING ADVENTURES

The constant stream of yelled 'support' from the bridge said it all. 'Get bloody stuck in, Clarko — come on, wind, mate, wind — this isn't some harbour fishing trip — COME ON, CLARKO!' And the advice: 'Seventy-five metres in front of us. See the shimmy? One o'clock. *One o'clock!* Come on, get it together, you're chilling out. I'm not chilling out. I'm excited! It won't matter what you throw in the water, they're gunna grab it! Come on Clarko, we're not fishing for trout now, mate! Throw the bloody thing at 'em!'

He's got two great deckhands, too: Daniel and Sally. You don't meet a lot of female deckhands, and even fewer deckhands as good as Sally Olafaatasi Asafo, which got us talking, because that much passion always comes from somewhere. Was it parents who were fishers, an uncle or even a teacher at school? No, with Sally there is a backstory like few I'd heard before.

When she was 18 she ran away to sea, heading off to see the world, only to be shipwrecked in the middle of nowhere. Wait for it . . . not for a week or two but for *two long years*. When fish is your only protein option on a deserted island, you tend to get pretty passionate about catching them! Now, as a father, you have to imagine this moment: after your daughter has been missing for two years, presumed dead, the phone rings and a familiar voice on the other end says, 'Hi Dad, it's me, Sal.' Hearing her recount a story that was obviously not shared often, speaking from the heart about her survival, was a very unexpected special moment indeed.

As I often remark, a fishing trip is never just about the fish you come home with, but the adventure of the day. The company you are in is a large part of that. Pulling away from the wharf in Hoppo's trusty launch, I knew we were in for a ripper.

As it turns out, Samoa was very much a sleeping giant when it comes to fishing. I held exactly zero expectations, so finding myself attached to a giant trevally (GT) on a popper less than 40 minutes after leaving the wharf at Apia came as a real surprise. When I say attached, it was literally heading for the horizon as if my 80 lb braided line was dental floss.

I told myself it was a fluke as I landed, weighed and released that 27 kg fish, then picked up my line and cast again. Bang, hooked up! It turns out that the reef up and down from Apia is alive with GTs, one of the most sought-after tropical game fish in the world. This was heaven! But my first catch wouldn't be the largest fish of the trip, not by a long shot.

I knew Hoppo was keen to show off the area, so on the way to our next fishing destination, he convinced me to put out some of his famous 'never fail' lures from his mate at JB Lures. Now I have 'pulled plastic' (the term salty fishing pirates give to trolling skirted lures for big game) many times, and the one thing I know is that you have to put in the hours to get a chance at a big fish. So I just thought this was something to do as we travelled between spots.

But it turns out that Samoa didn't get that memo. No sooner had we set a spread of 'special' lures, and with Hoppo settling into another bloody good yarn about bloody something or other, when one of the over-engineered Penn gold game-reels snapped into life. Its ratchet screamed blue murder, as whatever was on the other end played a game of 'how much line have you got?'. What it was wasn't exactly clear until, about 650 m of stripped line later, a shape exploded out of the water, leaving a car-sized hole.

All sorts of salty words started to flow subconsciously from Hoppo's lips, which I took to be encouragement, but could have been abuse,

Opposite above
Hooked up to my biggest blue marlin to date, off Upolu on Troppo Charters.

Opposite below left
A solid barracuda; good eating here in the islands.

Opposite below right
Skipper Greg (Hoppo) Hopping is finally happy with my performance with the rod.

All sorts of salty words started to flow subconsciously from Hoppo's lips, which I took to be encouragement, but could have been abuse, or perhaps even poetry.

or perhaps even poetry. To be completely honest, my sheltered, gentle upbringing meant I didn't even know what half of the words were, but that could just have been his thick Australian accent.

After a considerable period of shouting, winding, shouting and more winding, we finally caught and then released a blue marlin so large that based on length was predicted to have weighed around 170 kg. Poetically, the lure that caught it was called a 'dingo'.

Lures back in the water, including the dingo, and we had only just sat back down when the short rigger went off. This time it was a smaller fish that went deep straight away. Could this be a yellowfin tuna? Samoa gets more than its fair share of yellowfin and, sure enough, 10 minutes later a solid little barrel of a fish was in the boat iki'd and on ice for dinner later.

Please bear in mind this was all before we had even arrived at our 'proper' fishing spot. Here it went up another gear, catching everything from dogtooth tuna, huge coral trout and lots of other finned oddities that live only in warm water, such as the longnose emperor, a prized eating delicacy. It was a heck of a session, especially when given the chance to get in the water with my spear, where I nabbed a Spanish mackerel and a couple of barracuda for Sal to take back to her village to round out the day.

Having a debrief beer at a ramshackle bar next to the wharf that evening, Hoppo regaled us with talks of further offshore spots, where the fishing was even more impressive. I instantly started planning my next trip back, knowing I would never look at Samoa the same ever again. Fair bloody dinkum.

POISSON CRU AU LAIT DE COCO ET SASHIMI

POERANI DURAND
SERVES 4

1 kg fresh yellowfin tuna
1 bowl salt water
1 onion
1 carrot
fresh coconut cream, or
   1 can coconut cream
salt and pepper to taste

Tahitian sashimi sauce
2 teaspoons oyster sauce
1 teaspoon soy sauce
2 teaspoons mustard
2 cloves garlic
1 tablespoon canola oil
juice of 1 lime

To serve
fresh lettuce leaves
2–3 limes or 1–2 lemons

Cut the tuna into cubes for the poisson cru, and cut a plate of sliced tuna shoulder for the sashimi.

Place the cubes of tuna in the bowl of seawater to soak. While the fish is soaking, finely cut the onion and carrot and set aside.

After 5–10 minutes, drain the fish from the seawater and squeeze out any remaining water. Place in a bowl with the onion and carrot. Add the coconut cream and salt and pepper to taste, and mix.

Sashimi sauce

Place the oyster sauce, soy sauce, mustard, garlic and oil in a bowl. Hand-mix till smooth. Finish with lime juice.

To serve

Add the bowl of sashimi sauce to the sashimi plate. Line the raw-fish serving bowl with fresh lettuce leaves and pour the poisson cru au lait de coco over the top.

Just before serving, squeeze over the lime juice. (Note: Tahitian style is not to marinate the fish in lime first — it is added only minutes before serving.)

16

ONE FISH, TWO FISH

LOCATION
**GREAT BARRIER ISLAND,
NEW ZEALAND**

✕

FISH OF THE DAY
RED FISH

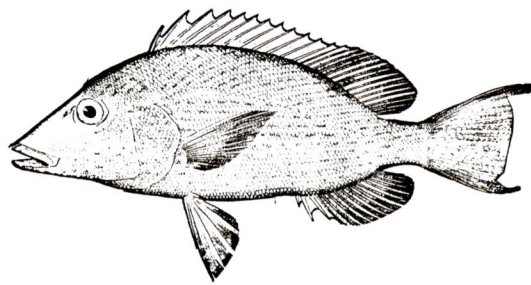

Colours play an important role in our lives. They can remind us of a place, a time of year, or a favourite thing. They can also shape the way we feel.

In Thai tradition, red is the colour for Sundays. In New Zealand the colour red led us to our first successful America's Cup campaign in 1995. Red in Chinese culture represents celebration and brings luck, prosperity, happiness and a long life. The question is: just how red can a fishing trip get?

I must have been to Aotea/Great Barrier Island a hundred times or more now, never having the same experience twice. On one of my more recent trips, I landed on the island with cameraman Steve Hathaway and his daughter Riley, of Young Ocean Explorers. We were off to film the nesting burrows of one of my favourite birds, the black petrel or tāiko, a real character of an avian that's one of our most endangered seabirds.

We had barely set foot on the island when a call came through that a pod of false killer whales had been spotted just offshore. False killer whales, like regular orca, aren't actually whales at all, but a type of large

Previous spread
Fish of the Day's Jeanneau 43 sits at anchor at Great Barrier Island, with Te Hauturu-o-Toi or Little Barrier in the background.

dolphin that are all black with small dorsal fins. They are sometimes also misidentified as pilot whales. There are several pods that show up around the New Zealand coast each year, when the water warms to around 19°C. Steve had spent three years tracking these mammals for the BBC's *Blue Planet*, so this was too good an opportunity to miss.

What followed was one of those special ocean days that occasionally just click into place. We managed to film these little-studied creatures as they mixed with bottlenose dolphins and tore schools of large kingfish to bits. Incredibly social animals, they swim in tight packs like a bunch of wriggling sausages. I came away thinking, however, that whoever lazily named them 'false killer whales' needs a sternly worded email — it would be the equivalent of us calling cats 'false dogs'. But then again, our most commonly stranded whale is called a 'pilot', so maybe there is a dark sense of humour amongst the cetacean-naming folk.

My day off the island ended swimming 'safety' for Steve amongst a pod of the dolphins. This is where I float with the cameraman, being the eyes in the back of his head and trying not to get in shot. This turned out to be quite useful as, thanks to all the kingfish blood in the water, a couple of large bronze whaler sharks showed up. The two swimming around us got progressively more and more curious, ending up with me having to give them a prod or two with my shark pole to keep them away. And when I say shark pole, I mean a simple piece of PVC pipe we use to keep sharks at a distance. Dealing with moments like that is an excellent way to make yourself feel truly alive — it certainly puts other trivial life niggles into perspective.

Usually, as the day fades it's time to return to port. That's one of the downsides of fizz boats — it's day trips only or uncomfortably close and uncomfortable sleeps at sea. Not so for this trip to the island; this was a self-contained affair. We had a 15 m Jeanneau launch at our disposal, plus we'd brought along an old friend with serious skills — chef Anthony McNamara. We wanted to target an Asian delicacy: anything red. Red seafood is highly sought after, especially in China, where red is the colour of happiness. Tasty

and happy is the ultimate combination. Our list therefore included scallops, surf clams, crayfish, snapper, red goatfish, pigfish and grandaddy hāpuku (also known as scorpionfish, and nothing like a regular hāpuku) — all tasty critters in their own right, but sharing that same colour trait. This is why we chose Aotea/Great Barrier Island as the location for filming this episode — we thought we could bag our colour-specific list in and around this incredible island without too much difficulty.

We started by getting our scallops and some surf clams on the western side of the island. After a bunch of failed spot dives to check the bottom we finally found a decent patch of scallops on an area of seabed that had not been ripped up by dredges. Scallops are becoming increasingly scarce around New Zealand as commercial fishers continue to dredge up the bulk of all catches. Over the past few years, scallop numbers have got so low that commercial operations are now only able to catch less than 10 per cent of what our quota management system (set up to protect species from overfishing) allows them. Many areas are closed to harvesting, and many more rāhui (closed seasons enacted by local Māori) are being put in place to try to counter the downward spiral of this species.

> **Red seafood is highly sought after, especially in China, where red is the colour of happiness. Tasty *and* happy is the ultimate combination.**

One of the main factors involved in their falling numbers is the way we catch scallops. By dredging the seabed, we destroy their habitat as well as the habitat for hundreds of other species. It is a method of harvest that simply has no place in modern fishing or, more importantly, modern sustainable fishing. If we want scallops in our future, we simply have to stop using dredges, both recreationally and commercially. The patch of scallops we found and harvested by hand was close to a reef, making it too risky to dredge. The rich, intact benthic crust around them was alive with other species, such as sponges and starfish, as well as being home to a thick bed of surf clams.

From there we headed around the top of Aotea/Great Barrier to Arid Island on the eastern side, to chase some of the other species on the list. When the weather is good, this place is a kaimoana treasure trove. Every bay and headland, sandy sea floor and reef is literally crawling with

Opposite above
Sitting at anchor in The Cove at Arid Island on the eastern side of Great Barrier Island.

Opposite below
A good-sized trevally taken on a kingfish jig. Not my target red fish so released to fight another day.

We decided that bringing along a chef might have to be the MO for all future trips — it certainly got us connected to our adventure in a more sensory way.

opportunity. We even had a visit from some of those bottlenose dolphins we had met earlier with Steve and Riley.

Fishing from our trusty liveaboard, we soon had an array of red species in the burley trail, from fat snapper to granddaddy hāpuku and pigfish. A quick snorkel saw our crayfish in the bag, along with a couple of goatfish — a fish the Hawaiians rate above most others for taste.

Every evening — and there were a few of them — saw us parked up in some picture-postcard bay as the sun set, with the rich aromas of Anthony's incredible cooking filling the salty, still air. We decided that bringing along a chef might have to be the MO for all future trips — it certainly got us connected to our adventure in a much more sensory way.

One of our primary motivations at *Fish of the Day* is letting people know about the things that lie, often unseen, on our doorstep. Through these snapshots of the destinations that we visit it has always been our intention to help people form more of a connection with the ocean around us. After all, it is a vital part of our economy, our culture, our lifestyles and our wellbeing. Making sure that what we enjoy today is around for generations to come, through acting as kaitiaki or guardians, is core to our beliefs.

And it is not just about what is under the water. Everything is connected, and on land at Aotea/Great Barrier there is also a veritable treasure trove of our most significant flora and fauna. Around 60 per cent of the island is set aside in reserves. The well-worn cliché that it's 'like stepping back in time' often gets pulled out, but maybe we've got that all wrong. Maybe this balanced nature utopia is where we should, as a nation, be headed. 'Stepping forward in time' is an analogy better suited to a proactive move towards a more sustainable, biodiverse and abundant New Zealand.

The healing properties of the prolific birdsong in the Glenfern Sanctuary at Fitzroy alone would do wonders for our collective stress. Off-grid living, using minimal resources, would put far less strain on the environment, while also reducing our emissions. Eating healthily off the land would result in reduced medical bills. And the sense of community you get from this place, complete with a few eccentrics, would make for a happier living environment. Forget looking back — let's figure out how to get more of this happening on the mainland now and in the future, for the good of us all.

Previous spread, clockwise from top left
Anthony McNamara fly fishing for snapper and kahawai off Great Barrier Island; Steve and Riley Hathaway heading out to film *Blue Planet*; Chef Anthony McNamara with our haul of scallops and surf clams; A blue shark comes in to take a closer look as we dive in open ocean; Anthony and I with an array of red fish, including snapper and red pigfish.

Opposite above
Another red fish — the well camouflaged and very tasty scorpion fish or grandaddy hāpuku.

Opposite below
Selective spearfishing in action — I decided to let this solid 20 pound snapper swim past. Big fish like this are essential for a healthy ecosystem.

CRAYFISH RISOTTO

ANTHONY MCNAMARA, LUXE
SERVES 4

1 medium-sized live crayfish
seawater for cooking

Crayfish stock
head and shell from 1
    medium-sized crayfish
1 onion, diced
1 clove garlic
1 carrot, diced
1 stick celery, diced
olive oil
fennel tops, if available
1 tablespoon tomato purée
pinch saffron threads
1 teaspoon coriander seeds
1 bay leaf
1 handful parsley stalks
1 tablespoon white
    peppercorns
salt
1 glass white wine
1.5 litres water

Risotto
1 shallot, finely chopped
2 tablespoons of olive oil
1 teaspoon sea salt
250 g risotto rice such as
    carnaroli, vialone nano
    or arborio
200 ml white wine
1 litre crayfish stock
    (see above)
100 g cold butter, diced
100 g grated Parmesan
juice of ½ lemon

To serve
1 tomato, diced
2 tablespoons chopped
    chives
olive oil
Parmesan

We've worked with Anthony since series one of *Fish of the Day*, when he shared a snappy little kahawai taco recipe (see pages 189–90) while cheffing at the Oyster Inn on Waiheke Island. Now he runs the luxury catering business Luxe. Anthony is not only a world-class chef, but he's also a mad-keen fisherman, which makes him perfectly suited to our show. Oh, and his recipes are next-level.

To cook your crayfish, first place it in a freezer — this will shut the crayfish down, effectively putting it into hibernation. Leave it in the freezer for 45 minutes while you bring a big pan of seawater to the boil.

If you don't have seawater, try to make the water you cook your crayfish in as salty as the sea. This will keep the meat of the crayfish sweet and tender.

Plunge the crayfish into the boiling water and simmer for 8 minutes for an average-size crayfish.

Remove from the water and leave to cool on a plate. Never drop shellfish into ice water to cool them down faster because this will make the meat tough and slightly bitter.

When cool enough to handle, twist off the head and reserve for the stock, then cut the tail in half with a heavy knife.

Remove the meat from the shell — easier to do when it's still slightly warm — and remove the intestinal tract, which will be a thin tube running through the middle of the tail, near the top. Chop the meat into bite-size pieces.

Crayfish stock

To make the crayfish stock, roughly chop the head and shell into pieces and roast in a hot oven for 15 minutes.

While this is roasting, sweat the chopped onion, garlic, carrot and celery in a little olive oil. Use a few fennel tops too, if you have them.

Add the roasted crayfish shells, tomato purée, saffron, coriander seeds, bay leaf, parsley stalks, tablespoon of white peppercorns, a little salt and a glass of white wine. When almost all of the liquid has evaporated, add the water, turn down the heat and simmer gently, without a lid on the pot, for an hour.

When the stock is done, pass through a sieve into another saucepan, pressing as much of the soft vegetables through the mesh as possible. Keep the stock warm to make the risotto.

Risotto

Sweat the chopped shallot over a medium heat in a little olive oil and the sea salt until soft and translucent, then add the risotto rice and continue to cook for a few moments, until the grains of rice also start to become a little translucent. Add the white wine and begin stirring the rice.

When all of the wine has been absorbed, start adding ladlefuls of the hot stock, waiting until each one has been absorbed before adding the next. Continue to keep stirring the rice all the time it's cooking; this will make your risotto nice and creamy.

After about 15 minutes' cooking, start tasting grains of rice: they should still have a bit of crunch in the middle, but as soon as you notice that the solid resistance has gone, the risotto is ready.

Remove from the heat and begin vigorously beating in the diced butter, grated Parmesan and a squeeze of fresh lemon juice to finish the risotto.

Check the seasoning, adding more salt if necessary. Also check the consistency of the risotto: it should not be too stiff or stodgy, but be slightly runny, like a good porridge. It will stiffen up while it rests, so don't be afraid to make it slightly runnier than you think it needs to be at this stage.

To serve

Serve the risotto into shallow bowls. Scatter with the diced meat from the tail, the chopped tomato and a few chopped chives.

Pour a generous amount of olive oil over the top of each risotto, and a little more shaved Parmesan.

17

ENJOYING
THE SUNSHINE

LOCATION
**SUNSHINE COAST,
AUSTRALIA**

✕

FISH OF THE DAY
FLATHEAD

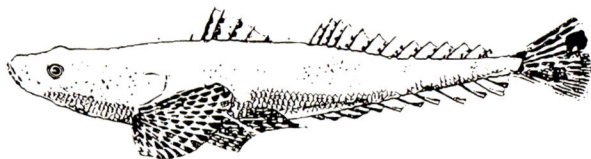

'One thing you can never do is choke a pelican.' There it was: the first of a bevy of ripper Aussie comments and advice dished out by retired ranger Michael McNamara aboard our Bill's Boat Hire pontoon craft. It only got better as the day went on, on our fishing excursion on a unique pumice-lined estuary with a name impossible to pronounce without letting your vocal assemblies slough into an Aussie aural interpretation. The road signs might read Caloundra, but it sounds a lot more like 'Cooolllooouunndrraaa' when the locals say it. And this trip was full of road signs, as we were on a road trip, after all, and keen to take in as much sunshine as the Sunshine Coast could beam down at us.

This is a beautiful stretch of Australia — more relaxed, more real and more true Aussie than its gaudy Gold Coast cousin down the road could ever hope to be. Lying to the north of Brisbane, it's littered with place names we all had fun with as kids: Mooloolaba; Maroochydore; Noosa; Eumundi; Boonooroo. It's also a place that winter seems to have forgotten all about. I was there in August, in shorts, in sunscreen,

Previous spread
The southern end of Rainbow Beach, just above Double Island Point, Sunshine Coast, Australia.

in 25°C. We enjoyed stunning, warm, clear-sky days mixed with the type of temperatures at night that lets sleep arrive easily. Perfect, really.

It's hard to put this place into words. Big comes to mind. There is a seemingly endless rolling hinterland, veined with mirror-rivers that flow towards linen-white beaches and a deep blue sea alive with fishy leviathans and bordered by endless dunes that crawl with dragons and wild dogs. 'Big' simply doesn't do this place justice.

I was here to chase a stubborn little fish called a dusky flathead. But floating about fishing with Michael and his hot pelican tips, my fish of the day was laying low, flat even. The highlights were soaring eagles and a crab hunt with a brush and shovel. Australia — where catching the bait is madder than a cornered platypus.

We needed these little soldier crabs for bait, or Michael did. I went for the trusty soft bait, as flathead are ambush hunters, sitting on the sand or buried in it, waiting for something edible to swim within striking range. But as the day slipped by, our bucket remained empty.

As Michael threaded another couple of soldiers onto his hook in the late afternoon sun, finally my soft bait found its mark and, after a pretty average fight, my just-big-enough fish of the day gave up at the boat and my reputation as a fisherman remained intact (just: it measured 41 cm, with the minimum size being 40 cm. Interestingly, though, to protect the breeding stock, the upper size limit is 75 cm — food for thought about some of our species here in New Zealand, perhaps?).

As luck would have it, I did spy a couple of fantastic specimens later in the trip, while underwater on one of Australia's best dive attractions: HMAS *Brisbane*. Purpose-sunk for divers in 2005, the ship was a Perth-class guided missile destroyer. She is an imposing sight, 133 m long, lying upright, bow proud in 28 m of water. Millions of dollars were spent stripping it of toxic materials and cutting holes for easy diver accessibility before it was sunk. It's a stunning dive, with marine growth and the ship's structure providing an island oasis in a large, sandy underwater desert off the Mooloolaba coast.

Following spread
Two juvenile humpback whales play next to the boat in Hervey Bay.

'One thing you can never
do is choke a pelican.'

— MICHAEL McNAMARA, RETIRED RANGER

It was along the side of its hull that I spotted the flathead I was seeking, laying low on the flats. The whole area is a marine reserve, which the flathead seemed to revel in, along with local stingrays, pufferfish and coral trout. Good on them. Our dive came complete with a soundtrack courtesy of some visiting humpback whales belting out the new-season whale song as they passed somewhere in the distance.

Did I mention it was warm? Here we were in the middle of 'winter' and the water was still sitting pretty at 21°C — that's peak summer water temperature in New Zealand. Luxury!

Further up the map, we entered the hipster end of the Sunshine Coast, Noosa. Winter Noosa is easily a thousand times better than summer Noosa, mainly because you've got so much more of it to yourself. Hidden amongst the smattering of eateries is a real highlight, Wasabi, which is hailed as one of the best Japanese restaurants in Australia. Chef co-owner Zeb Gilbert also runs the nearby Noosa cooking school.

After a good feed, we kept wandering north. For there lay a rendezvous with two of Australia's most notorious surfcasting specialists on a sandy island like no other. 'A Nugget, a Wazza and a Clarke get confronted by a dingo on the beach' sounds like the start of a questionable Aussie joke, but let me tell you, we weren't laughing when a growling dingo leapt into the back of the ute and started to rip off the previously secure lids of food containers. Australia — where you've got to watch the bloody dogs, mate.

To be fair, we were on the beach halfway down Fraser Island, in one of the last places in the world where packs of wild dingos roam freely. The island is a real Aussie treasure. The world's largest sand island, it is easily accessible via a short ferry ride to either end, or why not just land your plane on the beach? It's also a fun place to drive around in a 4WD. A real 4WD, that is — a school-run version won't cut it here. The photo board at our island accommodation suggested many a not-quite-good-enough vehicle had been claimed first by the soft sand and then by the tide. Australia — where everything is out to get you, even the sand.

As popular as it is for tourists, Fraser Island is also a great surfcasting destination, with a famous local tournament dedicated to a fish they

> **The highlight was a crab hunt with a brush and shovel. Australia — where catching the bait is madder than a cornered platypus.**

Opposite above
With guide Andrew Chorley and a monster cobia on a 20 lb line.

Opposite below left
Surfcasting for tailor on Fraser Island.

Opposite below right
Great armies of soldier crabs march across the sand flats at low tide in search of a meal.

call a tailor. Looking like a bulky, fat-headed kahawai, the mid-sized specimens are called choppers and big tailors are called greenbacks. My fishing companions, Wazza and Nugget, were so legendary at catching them that Nugget had been banned from all local competitions — at least that's what he told me as we cast lines from the shore into the night, sipping from his hip flask. Australia — where it's illegal to ruin a good yarn with the truth.

At 120 km long and just 24 km wide, the island acts like a long barrier to nearby Hervey Bay (pronounced 'Harvey' because, you know, it's Australia). Hervey Bay is home to some of the best fishing and wildlife in the country, thanks to its geographical location. Situated halfway between the warm tropical waters of the north and the cooler currents of the south, it collects all manner of life as a true marine convergence zone.

Australia — where the dogs are angry but the whales more than make up for it.

As if to prove this point, while pulling in a cool-water bludger trevally on light tackle, my rod doubled over and the braid began cracking off like it was touching power lines. Something had become determined to remove all of my line, after walloping and swallowing the fish I was initially winding in. Having just a 20 lb leader and using very light gear, I gave myself exactly a zero per cent chance of landing this mystery. But a back-straining hour and a half later, with more line-outs than a rugby match, we managed at last to bring alongside a fish they call a cobia.

Also called a black kingfish, they are a highly sought-after warm-water sport fish renowned for their fighting and eating qualities. They have an amazingly broad body and flipper-like pectorals, which gives them an unusual, almost shark-like look that creates huge resistance in the water. It took two of us to hold the fish up for a quick pic before placing it back into the water to watch it swim off strongly — the best part.

The bay is also a holiday destination for humpbacks returning north after feeding in Antarctica. On a single trip out we counted close to 50. At one fishing location, two whales were so insistent on playing with our stationary boat that I could smell their breath, and we had to eventually move away from them just to get a line back in the water. Australia — where the dogs are angry but the whales more than make up for it.

CHARGRILLED FLATHEAD AND SQUID-NOODLE SALAD WITH GENMAICHA FISH TEA

ZEB GILBERT
SERVES 4

400 g whole squid, tentacles reserved for the fish tea

1.5 kg whole flathead fish, filleted and skinned, reserving the frames for the fish tea

Genmaicha fish tea
reserved fish frame and squid tentacles
1 onion, chopped
1 stick celery, chopped
1 carrot, peeled and chopped
4 cm piece daikon, chopped
1 litre water
3 tablespoons genmaicha tea (green tea with toasted rice)
80 ml tamari soy
100 ml sake
60 ml mirin

To cook
3 teaspoons sea salt
1 tablespoon rice bran oil

Garnish
wild beach herbs, samphire, ice plant, etc.

To clean the squid, first remove the head, holding it behind the eyes and pulling it away (similar to taking the head off a prawn). Cut the tentacles off the squid just below the eyes.

Reserve the tentacles for the stock and discard the head.

Reach your fingers inside the tube and pull out the cartilage. Slice the tube along one side and open it up so it lies flat. With the back of your knife, scrape the inside of the tube to remove any remaining innards.

Turn the squid over and gently pull the skin away from the flesh, making sure to remove all the skin, including the two fins. Reserve the fins with the tentacles and keep the fish frames for making the fish tea.

Genmaicha fish tea

Rinse the fish bones and squid tentacles and place into a large pot. Add the chopped vegetables and water.

Bring to the boil, then reduce heat and simmer for 20 minutes, skimming any impurities from the top of the stock. Turn off the heat, add the genmaicha tea and allow to steep for 5 minutes.

Strain the stock. Add the soy, sake and mirin. To ensure the fish tea is well balanced between earthy, sweet and salty, add more soy for salt and more mirin for sweetness, adjusting to your liking.

Place the fish tea in a saucepan and ensure it is hot for serving.

Fish

With your squid in a sheet, slice as thinly as possible into long noodles. Simmer noodles in strained fish tea for 2 minutes.

Cut fish fillets into 200 g portions and season with sea salt and rice bran oil. Cook over charcoal, on a barbecue or in a fry pan: cooking times will vary depending on your method of cooking.

To serve

Pour squid noodles and fish tea into warmed bowls, top with fish pieces and garnish.

18

HOME

LOCATION
TAIRĀWHITI/GISBORNE,
NEW ZEALAND

FISH OF THE DAY
PINK MAOMAO

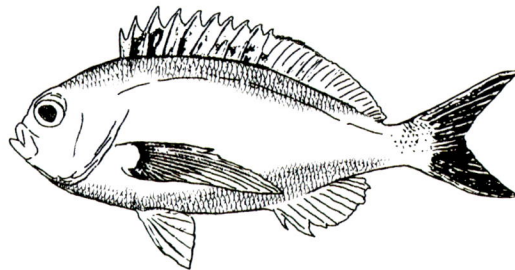

They say the isolation is the joy and the curse of this place. It might be difficult to drive to, but once you've arrived, it becomes even harder to leave.

Boasting the nation's best surfers and surf lifesavers, and with the second largest fishing club in the country, it's obvious that this place has a very special connection to the sea around it.

Growing up in Tairāwhiti/Gisborne, there are two land features that you become very familiar with: the Wharerata Ranges and the Waioeka Gorge, otherwise known as the main ways in and out. It took me years to realise that not everywhere in the country was accessed by such an onerous drive, and for a long time I thought that this geographical burden was holding my little city-that-wants-to back. 'If only it wasn't so tricky to get to, it could catch up to the rest of New Zealand,' I thought. Now, though, with the benefit of my years of travel and a bit of life under my belt, I've realised that this geographical isolation is actually one of the city's greatest assets. The rest of the country could do well to live more like they do in Tairāwhiti.

Previous spread
The Gisborne coastline, looking south from Pouawa Beach.

For a start, if it was any more laidback, people would not only have their arms out car windows, but their legs as well. How can you not feel instantly relaxed in a city known for residents shopping in their pyjamas? Chilled as, bro.

The pace of life here could almost be considered perfect, a pace that I still smile about when thinking of one childhood memory in particular: my dad driving up a side street to the main road (there is only one) and cursing his decision because it was 5 p.m. and the traffic was 'terrible'. Four cars and thirty seconds later we had a gap large enough to drive a convoy through, while Dad exclaimed how right he'd been, and 'what a mistake' it was to even think about navigating across town at that peak time.

So what is it that makes a whole city relax to the point where scuffs are considered formal footwear? Is it because it feels like a landlocked island, or that it's been blessed with great surf? Or is it the sunshine that rivals Nelson, or beaches better than Ōhope? Perhaps the fertile floodplains like the Hawke's Bay, wine equal to that of Marlborough . . . or is it the fabulous fishing? All the best things in life, it seems, are just down the road.

Imagine finishing work and being home or at the beach in under five minutes, and living in a place where you can indulge any hobby you want because of all the extra time you've been blessed with from not sitting in traffic. I grew up down here living inland on a small farm, but even then I could bike to the beach and get a couple of hours' surfing in before school each morning. Experiences like that shape who you become in life.

On this particular journey home, we had planned to shoot an episode around a species that grows bigger here than anywhere else in the country: the splendid-looking and -eating pink maomao. I had planned to try to catch one on rod as well as shoot one with the spear, the latter being a real challenge, as they are also nicknamed the widow-maker. This is because they have this uncanny ability to stay just out of range, while slowly forcing you deeper and deeper as you try to line up your shot.

It's funny how things work out: as it turned out, we just could not hook one. The problem was there were simply too many fish, and getting a bait to

Following spread
Dean Savage from Dive Tatapouri's tourism operation feeds stingray out on the reef at low tide.

'Marine reserves are great, but children don't necessarily get the opportunity to encounter animals. If you want children to get an empathy with the environment, they need to engage with it.'

— DEAN SAVAGE, DIVE TATAPOURI

these elusive neon-coloured beauties through the clouds of other species proved impossible. I did, however, manage to land a solid 30 kg kingfish.

Before we tried again, I wanted to catch up with a couple of old mates and talk them into giving me a little moral support for the spearfishing adventure to come. Tairāwhiti happens to have one of the best little tourist attractions in the country, run by one of those mates, Dean Savage. It's a short drive up the coast to where Dean and his wife Chris run Dive Tatapouri.

Dean and Chris have been a part of the local community here since forever, and they've been running Dive Tatapouri for over 20 years. Dean is a qualified skipper and a commercial diver, and his love of te moana has led him to running a business where connecting tourists and children with the ocean is what he is all about.

From what is basically a sea-shack on the seashore that houses waders, poles and guides to take you out onto the reef at low tide, in knee-deep water, the Dive Tatapouri team have tamed dozens of wild stingrays to come in and take food out of visitors' hands. Huge, friendly stingrays mix with massive kingfish that swirl between your legs, snatching at snacks, while on shore little blue penguins have burrowed under the shack. If you listen quietly in the kitchen you can sometimes hear them quarrelling under the floorboards.

This distinctly Kiwi experience gives visitors something that in Dean's words is increasingly harder to have these days, 'a direct connection to some raw nature', which he believes makes it easier for people to understand and so to care more about their environment. 'Marine reserves are great — they definitely play an important part in protecting our biodiversity and stuff — but children don't necessarily get the opportunity to encounter animals,' he says. 'If you want children to

Opposite above
Gisborne is well known for its crayfish or spiny red rock lobster.

Opposite below left
Dean Savage holds up the fish of the day, the neon-coloured pink maomao.

Opposite below right
A huge kingfish caught on jig off South Rocks in Gisborne.

get an empathy with the environment, they need to engage with it.'

'Keen on a spear tomorrow?' I casually asked him, after filming the stingray experience for the show.

'Absolutely!' Dean replied, without so much as a second of hesitation. So that meant it was time to find my other mate, Ross Gurau, who holds the world record for the biggest pink maomao ever speared, at 2.3 kg. I've known Ross ever since he wandered out of the bush one day for a spearfishing trip many years ago with Dean. He's a good, honest bloke and a bloody good spearo. Most days you'll find him walking Gisborne's northern beaches collecting washed-up seaweed. Ross is one of a bunch of 'seaweed gatherers' who work for AgriSea — a company that has embraced the value of seaweed as fertiliser and feed for the agricultural industry.

The problem was there were simply too many fish, and getting a bait to these elusive neon-coloured beauties through the clouds of other species proved impossible.

We headed out to a seamount about 20 km offshore — a single rock about the size of a small house. On this day it was an absolute millpond, which has its negatives — the water was so calm and clear we could see every shark for miles, and there were a few.

As we drove up on this underwater pinnacle, clouds appeared on the sounder, and on the edges of the clouds were bigger, more obvious shapes — kingfish, and lots of them. Ross and I were focused on the pinkies, but Dean had his extended whānau in town for Christmas, so his eyes were clearly on the yellowtail kingfish.

Getting into the water this far offshore, and particularly at this place, a little caution is always recommended, and within a few minutes the reasons became clear. First, a solid 2 m bronze whaler shark materialised

Opposite page
You can't feed the whānau with pink maomao, so we shot a couple of kingfish to keep everyone happy.

up from the depths. Shortly after this, a similar-sized mako cruised in on the surface to check us out. There would be no time to 'play fish' here — we needed to shoot them and get them into the boat a quick as we could.

After a couple of solid kingfish for Dean and some good pink maomao for Ross, it was my turn. Now the thing about pinkies is they sit deep, 20 to 40 m down, and as I said, they tend to draw you deeper and deeper as you try to line up your shot. It was at 25 to 30 m on this day that we got our opportunities and, if you're hanging at that depth waiting for one to come within range, time quickly becomes your enemy. This is why it's good to have an attentive buddy or two when you're hunting these guys, as a shallow-water blackout becomes a very real possibility. I used to be much more cavalier free-diving and pushing my limits when I could, spearing fish as deep as 30 m, but that blackout I experienced when chasing a huge dogtooth tuna in Niue (see page 115) made me re-evaluate my own personal limits.

On the first couple of dives I could see them, but they just kept moving deeper and just out of range, in typical pinkie style. On the next dive I shadowed the steep rock wall, which allowed me to slide closer, undetected. At around 22 m I finally got my chance. An hour or so later, and with a few kilos of premium kingfish and pinkies onboard, it was back to town and off to meet up with chef Tom Boyce to cook up our catch.

On this trip, like every trip that takes me back to Gisborne, I see more evidence of a town slowly waking up to its potential, but doing it in its own way. As an impatient adolescent I couldn't wait to get out of there; now, as an impatient Auckland driver, I spend a lot of that 'idle' time thinking about how I can get back in. Oh, to suffer that frustration my dad demonstrated in 'peak' local congestion. Yep, four cars in a row — such dreadful traffic!

CRISPY-SKIN PINK MAOMAO FILLETS IN KELP BUTTER

TOM BOYCE
SERVES 4

Kelp butter
100 g butter
dried kelp stems or kombu
   leaves
salt and pepper to taste
juice of ½ lemon

Tomato soup
6 large ripe tomatoes
umami salt
white pepper
olive oil

Lemon crème fraîche
2 tablespoons diced
   preserved lemon, or zest
   will also work fine
200 g crème fraîche
olive oil
salt and pepper

1 large pink maomao
   (approx. 1–1.5 kg)

Kelp butter
In a stainless-steel pot (as the lemon juice can draw metallic flavours from cast iron), melt the butter with the kelp stems. Simmer but don't brown the butter. Season with salt and pepper and lemon juice.

Tomato 'soup'
Roast the tomatoes in a hot oven until they are fully cooked. Place the tomatoes into a fine strainer and, using the back of a spoon, push the tomatoes through it, reserving the tomato juice. Season with the umami salt, white pepper and a little olive oil.

Lemon crème fraîche
Mix the lemon and the crème fraîche together with a little olive oil, and season to taste with salt and pepper.

Fish
Preheat oven to 250°C. Scale and fillet the fish, trying to leave the skin as intact as you can. Score the skin from side to side, and slice the fillets into the portion sizes you want.

Salt the skin side of the maomao and place into a hot, oiled frying pan, skin-side down.

Be prepared for the fillets to arch up, and be ready with a fish slice to flatten them as they seal.

Leaving the fish skin-side down, transfer the pan with fillets to the bottom shelf of the oven. Cook until you can see it is medium rare (just becoming opaque).

Remove from the oven and return to the element, over a low heat. Flip the fish and add the kelp butter. Using a spoon, baste the butter over the fish until you see milk releasing from the flakes and the skin is shiny.

Remove from the heat, but leave the fish to rest for a minute longer in the butter before serving.

To serve
Use deep plates or wide open bowls. Pour some tomato soup into the base of each bowl. Serve the pieces of fish skin-side up, and spoon the crème fraîche on top.

19

AT HOME IN HAWAIKI

LOCATION
HAWAII

FISH OF THE DAY
AMBERJACK

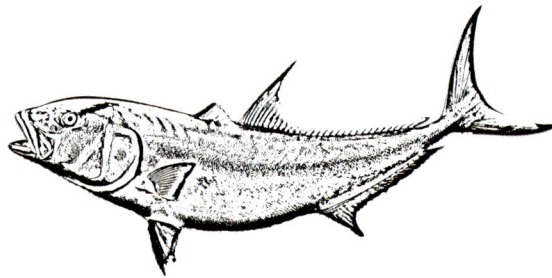

The similarities between the Hawaiian native language and te reo Māori are unmistakable. It always seems to be the most important words that travel best between islands over the centuries. It's probably why wahine (woman), wai (water), moana (ocean) and waka (canoe) are all identical in our culture and theirs.

The Hawaiian dialect uses a glottal stop, which in the word Hawai'i represents a dropped 'k'. When you put it back in, Hawai'i becomes Hawaiki. This name, as well as linguistic similarities like those listed above, has led many to assert that the ancestors of the Māori people came from the Hawaiian Islands.

These similarities of language is one tangible aspect that helps quantify the undeniable tingle of familiarity that you feel as a New Zealander in Hawaii. Perhaps it all adds up to part of the reason why Kiwis love the Hawaiian Islands — something luring us in that we can't quite put our finger on.

That connection is far stronger on the North Shore of Ohau, so distinctly different to the hotels and crowds of Waikiki. Take someone blindfolded to both and they'd swear they were on different islands.

Previous spread
Game-fishing Topshape charter boat, fishing for blue marlin off the Kona Coast, Hawaii.

It's a killer combination for those looking for a holiday that has the buzz of a big city combined with the laidback feel of a tropical island. By choosing which side of the island you stay on and which side you visit, you can select your own ratio of experiences based on your tastes.

The downside of these islands being such a tourist and retirement mecca, though, is food security. They say that if the cargo boats stopped coming to Hawaii, the islands would run out of food in just three weeks — and with nearly 10 million tourists a year to accommodate pre-Covid, it's easy to understand why. But with such incredible climate, scenery, action and lifestyle, it's no wonder that in normal travel times it's so popular.

We spent time on Ohau getting a feel for the island's true cultural roots and those undeniable connections we have to these islands. Both our cultures are committed to preserving the environment. In New Zealand we call this concept of guardianship and protection of the natural world kaitiakitanga; here in Hawaii it's known as kahu o ke kai. Looking after the marine environment is especially vital, because without a healthy environment, we wouldn't have fish to catch.

We visited some loko i'a on Ohau's North Shore — ancient fish ponds set up to ensure the local villages, during times of rough seas, still had fish to eat. To see these ponds being restored and used to create a sustainable food resource was reassurance that, like New Zealanders, Pacific Islanders are increasingly reconnecting with their culture and moving back into their roles as kaitiaki.

I was also lucky enough to be invited to a first-birthday lū'au while on Ohau. It's a bit of a big deal here in Hawaii, much like our twenty-firsts are at home. Part of the deal was assisting the family to collect the seafood for the party — the perfect job, really.

While catching the fish was relatively straightforward, the gathering of the octopus was a little more challenging — for me, anyway. This involved 'tickling' the octopi out of their reef lairs and then dispatching them using a traditional technique, one that involved biting them between the eyes — not exactly inviting.

From there we headed to the island of Hawai'i. I know, confusing. Locals have another name for it, which while it lacks imagination makes it easy to identify: they call it 'the Big Island'. Perhaps it's due to being overwhelmed by its 11 distinct climate zones. From deserts to rainforests, to frozen tundra juxtaposed against tropical reefs and warm ocean looking up to mountains capped with snow, it is quite something to take in.

It is, unsurprisingly, the biggest and youngest island in the whole Hawaiian group. It is so big that if measured from the sea floor it would be the highest mountain in the world, about 1.6 km higher than Everest! Not only is it the youngest, it's still growing, because it is made up of a group of very active volcanoes. Mount Kilauea oozed out another 283 hectares as recently as 2018.

Life on the Big Island is a double-edged sword. While destructive eruptions still occur, occasionally destroying roads and homes, the volcanoes are the island's number-one tourist attraction. There is a dramatic spike in visitors every time an increase in activity occurs, with some innate urge driving people to witness a bit of raw danger up close. My sightseeing helicopter pilot described it as 'the price you pay for living in paradise'. Thankfully these eruptions and lava flows are well forecast and slow moving. They are also a safe distance from the main tourist areas on the Kona Coast.

As a kid with my head stuck in fishing magazines and angling books, I knew all about the Kona Coast and its big-game fishing, particularly its spectacular big blue marlin fishery. It remains one of the only places in the world where you can catch 1000-pounders any month of the year. The wharves jostle with textbook big-game launches and character-perfect American charter skippers with names like Billy, Chuck and Mack.

I spent the day out fishing with Topshape Kona, in a 13 m Cabo launch kept in such immaculate condition that the glare off its pure-white decks had me squinting in sunglasses. The crew's attention to detail was so precise that they even had their own water-purifying unit on the jetty, solely

Opposite above
A lizard fish watches on as Joaquin Denolfo and I hunt for octopus for Joaquin's daughter's first-birthday lu'au.

Opposite below
Probably the craziest thing I've done while diving, dispatching octopus Hawaiian style with a bite between the eyes.

Following spread
A bucket-list dive off the coast of Kona. Night diving with a dozen manta rays.

'With an incredible 12 manta rays cartwheeling and pivoting about overhead, it became one of those moments you can spend a lifetime chasing. In Kiwi speak, "it was buzzy as, bro."'

— CLARKE GAYFORD

to wash the boat down without leaving a single watermark. Unfortunately, we returned from our day on the water chasing blue marlin without having any success.

I also embarked from this wharf on what I'd have to list as one of my top scuba dives of all time: night diving with manta rays. Just off the coast is a population of resident mantas that are drawn to the underwater lights that dive companies set up in crates on the sandy bottom, or shine down from paddleboards for snorkellers. The lights first attract all sorts of plankton then, from out of the pitch-black perimeter, the mantas swoop. These are *Mobula alfredi* reef mantas, the second largest breed of manta ray in the world.

To see them in daylight would be enough to get excessive bubbles free-flowing out of your dive regulator, but to have them materialise out of the pitch black is — well, I can only describe it as reminding me of that iconic scene from *Close Encounters of the Third Kind*. You know, that point where contact is being established with aliens through musical notes and flashing lights.

Here on the bottom, the bright shafts of LED light dance and pulse with microscopic life, creating a halo effect disrupted only by a creature that seems to defy any of Darwin's wildest daydreams. At up to 5 m across, with huge, cylindrical mouths sieving the lit-up clouds of protein, you'd expect them to be clumsy and slow to turn. Yet these colossal creatures have the grace and spatial awareness of your cat on dusk, when its eyes go black.

At one stage I was forced to lie flat on the bottom as they breezed above me maybe 10 cm away at most. On my first dive, with just three mantas, it was easily manageable. However, on the second dive, with an incredible 12 of these creatures cartwheeling and pivoting about overhead, completely blocking everything else from view, it became one of those moments you can spend a lifetime chasing. In Kiwi speak, 'it was buzzy as, bro.'

Opposite above left
The ancient loko i'a fish ponds on Ohau's North Shore.

Opposite above right
Inspirational aquaculturist Dr Neil Sims chatting about sustainability and food security in Hawaii.

Opposite below
Waiting for a bite off the Kona Coast.

Another interesting experience we had on the Big Island was checking out a chicken farm, and by that I mean the chicken of the sea. No, not albacore, but one of the most productive farmed fish in the world: kampachi or amberjack.

You see you can measure the output of a farmed animal by the volume you feed it versus what it produces by way of food. On land, the chicken rules supreme, with a ratio of close to 1:1. In the aquaculture world, tuna sits at around 28:1, meaning that you need to feed it 28 kg of other fish to get just 1 kg to eat. Salmon sit at around 1.7:1. Amberjack sits at a ratio of around 1:1, making it one of the most productive aquaculture species on Earth.

But add in the prowess and wacky scientist skills of Dr Neil Sims and you have the same fish eating a diet made almost exclusively of tofu, which lessens the impact on the ocean even more. Now that is the future.

Neil is originally from Australia, and has been here since 1990. He founded Ocean Era with American Michael Bullock, and together they are absolutely committed to solving the world's looming food crisis. His focus is next-generation technologies: how to feed the world and save the planet in the process.

'We want to soften humanity's footprint on the seas. We need to make this global shift away from terrestrial agriculture towards marine-based aquaculture without relying on getting more fish to feed to the fish. Essentially what we are trying to do is eventually turn these fish into vegetarians,' Neil says.

'We need to move towards more scalable forms of food production systems that have less impact on climate change. And that is what aquaculture is. Offshore aquaculture is an extension of that and the only way we can sustainably scale this.'

I loved Hawaii and Hawai'i — the water, the landscapes, the experiences — but the real gold here for those seeking immersion is the people. Mahalo!

Opposite above
A solid Hawaiian wahoo.

Opposite below
Where else in the world do the roads get swallowed by lava? A new no-exit on the Big Island.

TRUFFLE POKE

NAKOA PABRE
SERVES 2

0.5 kg fresh kampachi
  (kingfish or tuna will
  also do)
½ teaspoon sea salt
¼ red onion, roughly cut
2 tablespoons finely cut
  spring onions, plus extra
  for garnish
1 hot chilli
1 teaspoon diced
  lemongrass
2 tablespoons truffle oil
¼ cup shoyu (soy) sauce

Take your fillet of kampachi, kingfish or tuna and remove skin, any bones, red meat or sinew. Dice into cubes about 1 cm by 1 cm. I prefer this size rather than the bigger Hawaiian cubes as it's better for the kids.

Take the fresh cubes and add to a bowl with the sea salt. Dice red onion and spring onion and add to the fish along with finely chopped fresh chilli and lemongrass. Add the truffle oil and then the shoyu or soy sauce to taste. Add slowly as you do not want to over power or drown the poke. Mix well.

To serve, line a bowl with a banana leaf and add a generous serving of poke. Garnish with spring onions.

WHOLE KAMPACHI

NAKOA PABRE
SERVES 2

Chilli water
1 part vinegar
4 parts water
sea salt to taste
rough-cut chillies
mango purée (if you like a
  bit of sweetness)

1 whole medium-sized
  kampachi (snapper or
  tarakihi will also do),
  scaled but skin on
chopped spring onion

Chilli water

Combine the ingredients and let them sit until the liquid is properly infused with the chillies. Variations include adding slices of garlic and/or ginger (which you can also smash to release the juices more), as well as adding mango purée to make a sweet/hot version.

Fish

Cross-cut the fish skin to form 2 cm diamonds. Deep or shallow fry to crisp up the skin. If shallow frying, finish in the oven to cook through.

Serve the fish whole on a platter with dipping bowls of chilli water on the side. Sprinkle with spring onion and serve.

CRISPY-SKIN FISH WITH KAMOKAMO, CORN AND TOMATO SALSA AND KAWAKAWA HOLLANDAISE

JONO MARR
SERVES 4

Salsa

1 cob corn
8 x 2 cm thick slices of kamokamo
100 g garlic butter
3 tomatoes
handful baby spinach (optional)
1 tablespoon rice bran oil (or low taste oil)
salt and pepper, to season

Hollandaise

3 egg yolks
4 kawakawa leaves (stalks removed)
2 teaspoons white wine vinegar
1 teaspoon mild or wholegrain mustard
300 g butter
salt and pepper, to season

4 x 180 g white fish pieces with skin on
fresh herbs, to garnish

Salsa

Cook corn in boiling water for 5 minutes, then remove and place into iced water to stop the cooking process. Set aside. Repeat with the kamokamo, by boiling for 3 minutes before cooling in iced water.

Once cool, drain the water and place onto a roasting tray. Spread the garlic butter onto one side of the kamokamo.

Slice 1 tomato into quarters and remove the seeds. Dice remaining tomatoes and put into a bowl. Slice the corn off the cob and roughly chop the baby spinach, adding to the bowl with the oil. Mix and season to taste.

Hollandaise

Place egg yolks, kawakawa leaves, vinegar and mustard into a food processor — turn on high for a few minutes. Put the butter into a microwave-proof container with a lid (corner lifted on lid) and heat until the butter is boiling, approximately 3 minutes. With the food processor still going, slowly add the hot butter to the mixture. Season to taste and keep in a warm place until ready to serve.

Fish

Preheat a fan-forced oven to 200°C, or turn on chargrill or barbecue (if using a chargrill you can also use a hot pan).

Take the fish and score the skin with a few slices (to allow the fat to be released while cooking) and rub salt and pepper onto the skin. Cook the fish on a chargrill or a pan with oil, on high heat with the skin facing down. Once the side of the fish starts to go white, turn, then place in the oven for 5 minutes.

Place the kamokamo in the oven. Check fish after five minutes — you are aiming to cook it to medium; you don't want to overcook it or it will go dry.

Plating up

Place 2 pieces of kamokamo onto the plate on top of each other, then place fish on top. Spoon hollandaise onto the fish. Place a few spoons of salsa on the side. Garnish with fresh herbs.

20

TO EAT
CRAYFISH

LOCATION
**KAIKŌURA,
NEW ZEALAND**

✕

FISH OF THE DAY
BLUE MOKI

The road to Kaikōura is one of the most spectacular coastal drives in the world, with snow-capped mountains on one side and emerald-green ocean on the other. On this winding coastal highway you will see seals sunning themselves between hunts and, just offshore, dolphins leaping and playing among giant sperm whales.

But all is not as it seems. The kilometres of road works and strange white colouration on the coastal rocks hint at what this region has been through in recent years — one of New Zealand's biggest earthquakes, in December 2016. So severe was this 7.8 magnitude monster that it lifted the seabed over 2 m in places, as well as destroying houses and roads as it shook this place to bits. A no-take zone had to be established along the coasts after the earthquake as huge beds of pāua and seaweed and even crayfish colonies were destroyed when the seabed was violently pushed up and now need time to rebuild.

But even through all the pain that this place has suffered over recent years, you'll still find a happy-to-see-you, happy-to-help-you, happy-to-show-you bunch of locals who will always make this place extra special.

Previous spread
Surfcasting for blue moki at South Bay in Kaikōura.

An almost unspoken part of being a Kiwi is that, from a very young age, we convince ourselves that we are a small country tucked away in a quiet little corner of the world. But this mantra couldn't be further from the truth when it comes to describing our territorial waters. New Zealand's exclusive economic zone or EEZ (that is the 200 nautical mile zone around our islands) is one of the largest in the world. So when it comes to a share of the world's oceans, we are in fact an international heavyweight.

Rich upwellings from the deep here provide a food bonanza for living things both below and above the water.

Aotearoa has a longer coastline than mainland China, and a wonderful chunk of significant continental shelf that oozes out from the edge of our coasts. Nearly everywhere this underwater layer of crust extends many miles offshore before dropping sharply away into the abyss of open ocean, thousands of metres deep. Nearly everywhere, that is, except for a place whose name translates as 'to eat crayfish': Kaikōura. Here the shelf angles in to a pinch-point, coming dangerously close to the land. While this all might sound like an abstract paragraph on geography, let me make the argument that the significance of Kaikōura's place in the world is largely because of this very feature.

Early Māori and intergenerational fishers have long known of the attributes created by this vast underwater canyon, almost as deep as the mountain range of Kaikōura is high. Rich upwellings from the deep here provide a food bonanza for living things both below and above the water.

This contrast of deep water very close to shore makes it the perfect restaurant for sperm whales, who are present off Kaikōura year-round, making the town the most reliable place in the world to see them. Oceanic currents push nutrients up from over 1000 m deep, creating an ideal environment for thousands of dusky dolphins, too. Duskies are night hunters, so during the day the large pods sleep, play and socialise on the surface, making this a perfect place to experience them close up as well.

Above the water it's a seabird free-for-all, the pecking order firmly

established by size and reputation. Basically, the natural order of scavenging priority goes like this: albatross, then giant petrel, then shearwater, then cape pigeon. But we're not talking about just one species of albatross: Kaikōura is known to be visited by 18 of the world's 24 species. When it comes to seabirds, New Zealand is an international heavy-hitter and this place is a real focal point.

The reason I've highlighted whales, dolphins and seabirds is that the abundance of all three has been harnessed by tourist activities, and it is these that have really helped put Kaikōura firmly on the travel map. It's not just a flash in the pan, either, charters catering to watching and swimming with whales and dolphins have been operating here for over 30 years, this longevity a key indicator of the quality of the experience. These sustainable activities match my own mantra of finding positive ways to connect people to the sea, so that they will care more about the ocean in the future.

While whales and seabirds are a definite attraction, we were in town on this trip to chase blue moki. Initial attempts at getting them surfcasting off Kaikōura's beaches were unsuccessful. And when the rod and reel isn't working for me, then it's time to pick up the speargun and get wet.

I was being guided by local Hunting & Fishing guru Bryn Williams, who said he knew a spot: a shore dive on the peninsula, just a hop, skip and a jump from town. We swam out about 100 m and sure enough, there they were. A narrow gut in the rocks was loaded with a dozen or more perfect eating-sized blue moki. There is a lot to be said for using local knowledge, and this was a good example. We hadn't seen a single blue moki all trip, and now we had plenty.

Of course, you can't come to Kaikōura and not eat crayfish. If you can't catch them yourself, the place to go is Nin's Bin, which, at first look, seems

There is something special about sitting at an old picnic table, being hit with a salty, wet, seaweed-infused breeze blowing off the very water where your meal has just come from.

Opposite above
A feed of crayfish from Nin's Bin.

Opposite below
Wild-food forager Peter Langlands talking about albatross in the Kaikōura region.

Following spread
Surrounded by dusky dolphins. One of the best dolphin encounters in the world.

to be just a caravan on the side of the road. But there is a good reason that Lonely Planet called this one of the world's top food experiences, listing it at #7 out of 500 on their Ultimate Eatlist in 2018. It's the totality of experience that sets Nin's apart. Let's be honest — crayfish can be found in plenty of flash restaurants at flash prices, but there is nowhere quite as picturesque as Nin's Bin.

Nin's is now run by Johnny Clark, the grandson of the man who set it up in 1977, Ronald Clark. Johnny can be found most calm days in his boat right out in front of Nin's, working his craypots. Customers are often treated to the sight of the boat being hauled by tractor past their lunch table as Johnny drags more crays up to the big custom boiling-pots across the road.

The location itself could not be more perfect, with the caravan looking out over the coast and the Kaikōura Ranges looking down from above. Smell is a sense we often experience subconsciously, and there is something special about sitting at an old picnic table, being hit with a salty, wet, seaweed-infused breeze blowing off the very water where your meal has just come from. For me that is the icing on the cake. These elements together become part of this food experience, and the very reason Nin's has been so popular locally and internationally all these years.

Sadly places like this are rare; Nin's only exists because Johnny's grandfather was wise and hung on to his crayfish quota. It now costs over a million dollars to own a tonne of crayfish quota, and almost all the spiny red rock lobsters (crayfish) harvested in this country are sent to China. I know New Zealand chefs who refuse to serve it now because of the way they feel squeezed out of the market.

A lack of access to fresh local New Zealand seafood is a huge complaint of many of our restaurant owners, who struggle to source fresh fish from

I believe we are heading into an exciting era of New Zealand's culinary journey, and I believe in the coming decades we will really start to develop a proper sense of what a taste of this country actually is.

Opposite above
Fishing for blue cod with Kaikōura Fishing Tours, with the Kaikōura Ranges in the background.

Opposite below
Dusky dolphins circle the camera in the cold waters off Kaikōura.

their area. It's part of the reason why we are starting to see innovation, with dishes like aged kahawai, baked butterfish heads, cured albacore, pickled pilchards and kina chawanmushi all popping up on menus. It's a case of chefs taking what local produce they can get fresh and bringing a whole new twist to previously overlooked kaimoana.

I believe we are heading into an exciting era of New Zealand's culinary journey, and I believe in the coming decades we will really start to develop a proper sense of what a taste of this country actually is. It's my great hope that places like Nin's become the norm and not the exception as we develop not just our national food identity, but our local regional specialities as well. All we need is there to be fish in the water to catch and the return of small artisanal fishermen and families like Johnny's.

Above
One of just a handful of banded dotterel left in Kaikōura — the population has been decimated by cats.

CRAYFISH AGNOLOTTI

ROB CULLEN
SERVES 4

1 medium-sized crayfish
250 g white fish

Tomato water
6 vine-ripened tomatoes
  (the riper the better)

Agnolotti
10 eggs
250 g flour
salt
zest of 2 lemons, juice of
  ¼ lemon
100 ml cream
salt and pepper to taste
piping bag
fluted pasta wheel

To serve
good-quality olive oil
wild greens: wood sorrel,
  mustard flower, ice plant,
  watercress, fennel fronds

Tomato water

Crush the tomatoes and place in a cheese cloth-covered sieve over a collection bowl overnight in the fridge to allow the clear water from the tomatoes to collect. You can speed up the process by squeezing them through the cloth.

Agnolotti dough

Combine 9 eggs and flour with a dash of salt and knead or use food processor until dough forms. Roll out to form sheets.

Crayfish

Kill the crayfish by first chilling it down in a freezer or ice slurry of -1°C then placing a knife lengthways through the shell behind the eyes.

Boil the crayfish for 6 minutes.

Cut the crayfish tail into chunks and separate leg and shell meat along with the crayfish mustard (stomach contents) and set aside.

Agnolotti filling

Add crayfish offcuts and mustard to blender with fish, lemon zest and juice. Add white of one egg and 50 ml of cream and blend to form a paste. If too thick add more cream. Season with salt and pepper to taste.

Agnolotti

Add filling to piping bag and pipe a 1 cm line of mixture down the pasta sheet. Fold the pasta sheet over and seal the edge and ends. Pinch the pasta with your fingers to form 1.5 cm long packets of filling. Using a fluted pasta cutter, cut the edge and in between the parcels to form rectangular pockets. Then fold the flat edge up to bond with ends of the parcel and flatten the bottom so they sit upright. Poach in boiling water for 3 or 4 minutes until they float to the surface signalling they are cooked.

To serve

Heat the tomato water and add to a wide bowl, and add a tablespoon of olive oil. Place the agnolotti into the tomato water. Garnish with a generous amount of wild greens and place the chunks of crayfish on the top, season and serve.

21

HIS HIGHNESS
THE SHYNESS

LOCATION
AITUTAKI, COOK ISLANDS

X

FISH OF THE DAY
BONEFISH AND KUTA
(RED SNAPPER)

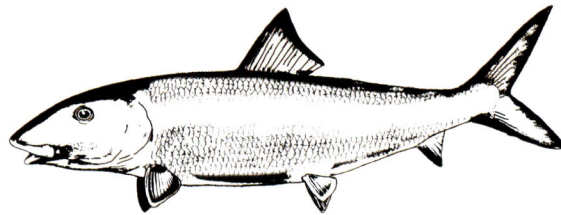

I went to Aitutaki specifically to test my skills against a fish that, owing to its speed and shy nature, which make it difficult to catch, has more nicknames than almost any other fish in the world. They call it bones or the phantom, the silver bullet or the grey ghost, the torpedo of the flats, but far and away my favourite is 'his highness the shyness'.

For the uninitiated, bonefish are the world's number-one target for saltwater fly fishers. Around the world it is said that fishers spend more money chasing bonefish than they do marlin, such is its revered status. And the Cook Islands atoll of Aitutaki is surrounded by a remarkable bonefish fishery, with an amazing backstory.

There are 15 major islands in the Cook Islands group, scattered over a massive part of what really can only be described as the blue continent. Most people are familiar with the largest island, Rarotonga, but outside of this, what else is there?

The second most visited island is Aitutaki, just an hour's flight from Raro. Prior to Covid, Aitutaki had increasingly been popping up on travellers' radars, yet visitor numbers remained low enough to not take away any of its magic. And magic it is, with Lonely Planet once voting it as the world's most beautiful lagoon. It is also one of the world's largest ringed lagoons and, at just 7 m deep, it's a snorkellers' and kite-boarders' paradise.

If Rarotonga is the Cook Islands' Auckland, then Aitutaki would have to be the Bay of Islands. Its idyllic tropical setting, with the mandatory palms, white-sand beaches and warm, calm waters, blends perfectly with the 2000 locals. Having a laidback lifestyle is so important here they've even banished all dogs after one bit a chief's daughter. (As an aside, this has given the local cats a huge confidence boost, and you can regularly see them down at the beach hunting small fish in the water under the moonlight.)

But it was the bonefish that I was here for — a fish that has a big history in these waters. For generations, locals netted and ate the bonefish in the lagoon in large numbers. But through the assistance of some visiting sports fishermen, who quickly realised what amazing specimens were here and what an opportunity that presented, they helped to facilitate a complete transformation.

Instead of netting the fish, locals were trained to become guides. They were given special boats and poles to manoeuvre silently across the flats, and taught how to target the fish for visiting anglers. This quickly developed into one of the island's best income-earners. The money generated through fishing fees goes directly back to locals who, while unsure at first, took a chance and had their risk pay off. It's been so successful the bonefish are now protected, and all are released after capture. The result is a win not only for the fishery, but a big win for the residents as well.

I spent my first days here perfecting my casts. We had only a few days with world-renowned bonefish guide Itu (pronounced E-two) Davey, and I didn't want to waste it.

Itu has a gift. I have always thought that I have good eyes when it comes to spotting fish, even from some distance, but finding and stalking a fish like the bonefish requires next-level eyesight. Itu would be pointing out multiple fish cruising around and I wouldn't be able to make them out until

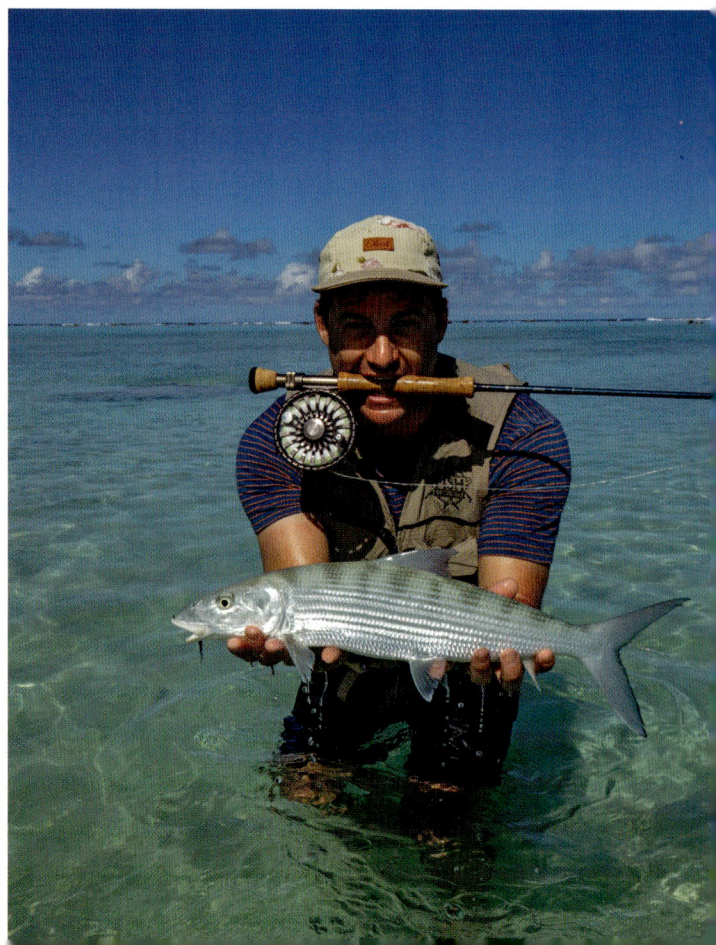

FISH OF THE DAY   269

Finding and stalking a fish like the bonefish requires next-level eyesight. Itu would be pointing out multiple fish cruising around and I wouldn't be able to make them out until they were virtually at my feet.

they were virtually at my feet. Casting to them was about Itu calling distance and numbers on the clock for direction. He could even see the fish turn and strike before I even knew I was onto one.

Getting one to the boat (or to your feet if you're wading) was a lot harder than I thought it would be. 'Two o'clock, two o'clock, ten metres, moving left,' came the call from Itu. I was casting blind; I simply couldn't see the fish he was getting me to cast to. 'Longer, longer . . . right there. Retrieve, retrieve — faster, faster — STRIKE!' And just like that I was hooked up to a freight train of a bonefish.

The line peeled off the reel as I tried to keep pressure on it. 'Higher, get your rod up!' came the call, but before I could respond to Itu's commands the fish ducked behind a coral head. As soon as the line touched the razor-sharp coral, it broke. These mullet-looking beasties are far more powerful and speedy than I had ever dreamed. Bonefish 1, Clarke 0.

For the whole rest of the day we cast at invisible fish with no luck. They simply weren't feeding in the heat of a cloudless and outrageously hot day. Finally we jumped out of the boat and waded across the sand flats. We were down to our last cast when finally one showed an interest in my fly. This time there were no coral heads to hide behind, and after a solid 10-minute battle I was in the bonefish club. Having learned first-hand, I truly understand why anglers the world over revere this fish.

Now, it is not often that you get a chance to spend a whole day with the Prime Minister of a country — and, no, I'm not talking about New Zealand. But here in Aitutaki we were lucky enough to be joined by Prime Minister Henry Puna to fish off the boat and talk about the significance of the reserve that he had helped put in place around his blue continent. Marae Moana is extraordinary in its size, spanning over 2 million sq km, and its vision: all fishing activity is now strictly controlled, including a

Opposite above
My spearfishing haul of parrotfish and kuta, freshly gutted and scaled for the Prime Minister of Cook Islands' dinner.

Opposite below left
Bonefish guide Itu and I pole our way quietly across the lagoon in search of the quarry.

Opposite below right
After plenty of near misses, it finally all came together to land a bonefish.

'We were brought up to conserve — we take only what we need for the day or for a couple of days. We don't take too much because we believe in leaving enough in the ocean for the next time.'

— HENRY PUNA, COOK ISLANDS PRIME MINISTER 2010–20

50 nautical mile zone around each of the 15 islands, where no commercial fishing is permitted. It is one of the biggest marine-protected areas in the world and has started a big shift in the Pacific.

'For me, especially as Prime Minister, the challenge is to preserve as much of this as I can for the future generations,' Henry told us. 'And I think, by tradition and by nature, the people of Aitutaki and the Cook Islands are very conservation-minded. Conservation is part of our nature. You know, we were brought up to conserve — we take only what we need for the day or for a couple of days. We don't take too much because we believe in leaving enough in the ocean for the next time. And that's a wonderful conservation principle to practise. I have absolute faith in the conservation measures we have in place.'

Pacific Islanders truly understand the value of their primary protein source, and falling fish numbers have been ringing alarm bells for some time. First to bring about massive change was Palau, which placed 80 per cent of its exclusive economic zone (EEZ) into a reserve. Niue has followed, with 40 per cent of its waters now protected. Today, countries like the Cooks are leading the way. Reducing our commercial take of fish means more fish in the water, and that is food for the future.

If we could all take a leaf out of these islands' environmental planning and foresight books, we might be able to protect our food sovereignty for future generations. After all, this is why the idea of the EEZ was officially sanctioned by the UN in 1982. It gives each country a chance to protect the valuable resources on their doorstep for the future, even though in many places it did little to slow wholesale domestic exploitation of them.

I could have talked all day with Henry about this, but he specifically asked for fish for tea — and a particular personal favourite fish — so over the

> **Reducing our commercial take of fish means more fish in the water, and that is food for the future.**

Previous spread
The dive boat is made to feel insignificant on the outer edge of the reef as I spearfish for kuta.

Opposite above
Guide Itu carefully searches the surrounding lagoon for signs of 'his highness the shyness'.

Opposite below
The perfectly white-washed Cook Islands Christian Church and graveyard on Aitutaki.

COOK ISLANDS CHRISTIAN CHURCH ARUTANGA AITUTAKI

MAIN SERVICE

CICC

SUNDAY MORNING — 10AM
EVENING — 5PM

DAWN SERVICE
WED FRI SUN — 5.30AM
SUNDAY SCHOOL — 3PM

PSALMS 119:105
Your word is a lamp to my feet and a light for my path.

side I went, speargun in hand. I had a vague idea of what it was he wanted, based on his description — a kuta or red snapper. Poking my head into a few caves, I found what I was looking for, but was then suddenly chased out of the water. Not by a shark — no, worse. This was the biggest moray I had ever encountered, and it was intent on relieving me not only of my catch but a limb or two as well. Chasing me over the reef, it took a lot of frantic kicking with my flippers at its open mouth as it tried to latch on. Not an experience I'll forget in a hurry!

Later that day, sitting on the deck at our accommodation under a perfect sunset, Henry and I continued our chat about food security, the importance of culture and our mutual commitment to the generations to come. As for the kuta — well, after eating one I now understand why they are Henry's favourite fish. Delicious.

Marine conservation planning is something readily embraced by the people of the Cooks, and Henry is incredibly proud of their work. And if the result is being able to get into the water in places like Aitutaki and swim with schools of giant trevally, or chase bonefish on the flats, then it has all been worth it.

SPICY PAN-FRIED FISH

THOMAS KOTEKA
SERVES 2

Rub
3 tablespoons Best Foods
 mayonnaise
1 tablespoon chopped sun-
 dried tomatoes
1–2 tablespoons chopped
 lemongrass
fresh chilli (to taste)
1 teaspoon mustard
2 tablespoons diced
 pineapple
2 tablespoons fish sauce
squeeze of lemon

1 whole fish (approx.
 1–1.5 kg), gutted and
 scaled
salt and pepper
clarified butter
olive oil
1 clove garlic, sliced

Add all the ingredients of the rub to a bowl and mix together. Season fish with salt and pepper and score the skin with cuts 2 cm apart on both sides.

Heat some clarified butter and olive oil in a fry pan on medium to high heat (clarified butter has a higher flash point, so you can get good heat out of it without it burning). Place the fish into the pan and ladle oil and butter over it. After 1 minute add sliced garlic.

As the fish begins to open up, drain most of the oil and butter from the pan, and add the rub to the fish while still in the pan, turning the fish to coat both sides.

Once the fish is cooked, remove from the pan and serve.

22

THE SUPERVOLCANO

LOCATION
TAUPŌ, NEW ZEALAND

✕

FISH OF THE DAY
RAINBOW TROUT

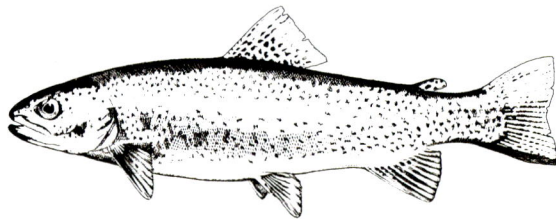

At over 600 sq km, Taupō is one of the largest lakes in the Southern Hemisphere. It's deep, too — in places over 150 m to the bottom. But it is more than just a lake: it is an enormous volcanic crater. Its last flurry of life, just 1800 years ago, was such a violent eruption that it turned the skies red in ancient China, it was recorded in Rome, and ash from it has been found not only down in Antarctica but all the way up in Greenland as well. It was the most violent eruption the world has seen in the last 5000 years!

Lake Taupō also has a reputation for producing some of the biggest trout in the world. Maybe this trip would see me gain my membership of the double-figure club.

Ten pounds, or just 4.5 kg: I mean, how hard can it be to catch a fish of that size? It doesn't sound like a big number, but in the trout-fishing world it is the ultimate. Joining that elusive double-figure club was proving far more challenging than I ever thought. I live in New Zealand, the home of giant trout, so surely if I was going to join that club anywhere in the world, it should be here? Maybe Taupō would deliver.

Previous spread
Chasing rainbow trout with guide Louie the Fish on a secret lake in the Taupō district.

We had three things on the list for this trip, and one required a speargun. Yes, a speargun in trout country . . . but don't worry, I'll fill you in when we get to the other end of the lake.

First up, we made a visit to some of the thermal hotspots. We started our Taupō experience at a place called Ōrākei Kōrako, meaning 'place of adornment' — a place Lonely Planet named as the best thermal area in New Zealand. Walking the trails through the vast network of geysers, turquoise-blue hotpools and bubbling mud, I was struck by the vibrant palette of colours. The oranges, neon yellows, greens and blues seemed almost Photoshopped onto the landscape. And you can't help but feel vulnerable here, on the edge of this cracked crust where the Earth's inner fury bubbles relentlessly to the surface.

The next stop heading south was another thermal wonderland, this time Wairakei, home to the first geothermal power station of its type in the world, which utilises flash steam from geothermal water as an energy source. Built in 1958, the station still delivers power to the New Zealand grid. But what I came here for was a fishing operation made possible by a by-product of the station. Since the 1980s, hot water has been piped from the plant to create the Huka Prawn Park, where giant Malaysian river prawns are commercially farmed.

It's quite fascinating: the male prawns are born with this golden claw, and that's their fighting claw. With that golden claw, they're pretty much out there scrapping with all the other males. However, if they become particularly good at fighting and become the crown prince of prawn battles, their golden claw changes colour to blue, which is for the ladies. So if you're a blue-clawed prawn, you have risen above the gold claws, and you get to go out and have your pick of all of the lady prawns. Who knew?

Prawn-star romance aside, I mentioned I had a speargun with me. I had timed this trip to coincide with a spearfishing competition that

> **If you're a blue-clawed prawn, you have risen above the gold claws, and you get to go out and have your pick of all of the lady prawns. Who knew?**

Following spread, clockwise from top left
Louie with a nice rainbow trout; Louie the Fish fly fishing for trout on the Tongariro River flowing into Lake Taupō; A speared brown bullhead catfish in Lake Taupō; Our catch of rainbows — dinner is served; It doesn't get much prettier than this — Louie's secret trout lake not far from the shores of Lake Taupō.

happens once a year, but obviously it's not for trout. There is an invasive pest that is running amok here — the brown bullhead catfish. The annual catfish cull takes place out of the Motuoapa Boating Club, down the southern end of Lake Taupō, and on a good day this wee competition can relieve the lake of close to 4000 of this nuisance fish.

Spearfishing for them is tricky. The best place to spot the fish is on the edge of the weed line, in 12 to 15 m of water. They're often just under the edge of the weed, fossicking around for invertebrates to eat. Once you get your eye in, the pole spear makes light work of them. And while most end up as compost, they are actually incredibly tasty little treats so it is worth cooking a few up in celebration of your contribution to maintaining the health of the lake ecosystem.

Ten pounds, or just 4.5 kg: I mean, how hard can it be to catch a fish of that size? It doesn't sound like a big number, but in the trout fishing world it is the ultimate.

It's for that same reason that I don't mind keeping caught trout rather than releasing all of them. You see, trout are a bit of an anomaly in the conservation landscape of New Zealand. As an introduced fish they are actually a hugely invasive pest species which has done irreparable damage to native fish species throughout the country, yet we treat them like royalty. (It surprises many people to learn that rainbow trout even feature in the top-100 list of the world's most invasive fish.) Perhaps this is a legacy of colonisation and the esteem in which they were held by the aristocracy of mother England.

In New Zealand they cannot be bought or sold commercially, and seeding programmes — the release of fingerlings that have been bred in captivity — are active right around the country, in effect maintaining this animal's stranglehold on what is left of our native freshwater fish. On top of all of that, there are strict rules for those who pursue them recreationally — rules that have even seen a few Taupō locals face jail

Opposite above
One of the many trout-rich rivers that flow through the Taupō district.

Opposite below
While there are plenty of rainbow trout in the rivers over summer, they can be hard to catch.

time for poaching. Juxtapose that against the minimal rules around the harvesting of native whitebait, of which *all* species that make up our fritters are considered endangered, and you start to see the odd relationship we have with trout.

To catch a rainbow or two for dinner, and in pursuit of my seemingly endless quest to join the double-figure club, I enlisted the help of one of Tūrangi's best-known trout aficionados, a chap by the name of Louie the Fish. Louie (real name Louie DeNolfo) was born in Connecticut in the US, but pre-Covid he spent half his time in Tūrangi and the other half in Hawaii.

Louie the Fish, I would have to say, is one of the most colourful characters in the trout-fishing scene. He is the only fly fisher I've seen that can play flawless blues harmonica at the same time as catching a trout. And he's influenced the way we catch them here in New Zealand, too. He was the first to introduce the Glo-bug and silicone smelt style of bottom fishing for trout here, and not without a little resistance from the old guard, I must say. When he's in-country you will often find him at the bridge pool plying his craft, or back in his garage carving beautiful bone and pearl-shell fish and fish hooks.

As an introduced fish, trout are actually a hugely invasive pest species which has done irreparable damage to native fish species throughout the country, yet we treat them like royalty.

Louie the Fish knows his stuff, but it was the middle of summer, so the rivers proved slow for fishing on this trip. In pursuit of that elusive 10-pounder, we were forced to visit a couple of his 'secret' small lakes on Taupō's edges. Sitting mid-lake in Louie's tinnie, we caught no shortage of fish as Louie belted out his signature trout-raising rifts on his harmonica and we flicked Woolly Buggers or drifted Glo-bugs across the lake floor. But, alas, no monsters . . . again. The frustration continued to mount. How could a fish I used to care so little about so quickly become my freshwater dogtooth?

WHOLE RAINBOW TROUT WITH PRAWNS AND CONFIT POTATOES

GARY SAVAGE
SERVES 4

1 whole rainbow trout
(approx. 1.5–2 kg)

Marinade

2 tablespoons
Worcestershire sauce
juice of ½ lemon
½ glass white wine
2 tablespoons mustard
(to taste)
1 teaspoon beef bouillon
liquid or ½ teaspoon
powder
lemon pepper
few slices fresh ginger
1 onion
handful parsley
4 sprigs thyme
salt and pepper

Potatoes

12 baby potatoes
oil
rock salt

Butter sauce

½ cup cream
200 g butter

Prawns

8 large prawns
flour to coat
butter to cook

Fish marination

Gut and scale the trout, and remove the gills. Make 3–4 vertical cuts each side along the length of the fish's body, down to the bone, and place it in an ovenproof dish.

Combine the Worcestershire sauce, lemon juice, white wine, mustard and beef bouillon. Add a sprinkle of lemon pepper and a few slices of fresh ginger.

Roughly slice the onion and parsley and place over the fish. Pour marinade over and into the fish, rubbing it into the flesh. Add a bit of fresh thyme and season with salt and pepper. Place into the fridge and marinate for several hours or longer.

Potato baking

Wash potatoes and drizzle with oil and rock salt and bake at 180°C till cooked (about 45 minutes to 1 hour).

Fish baking

Preheat oven to 160°C. Take the marinated fish out of the fridge and sit fish upright as if it was swimming. Bend the fish around into a semi-circle. Hold its shape in place by tying some string to its tail, with the other end through its jaw.

Place back into the marinade and cover in aluminium foil. Cook for approximately 20 minutes, adjusting cooking time according to the size of the trout.

When cooked, remove from the oven and stand for 10 minutes.

Butter sauce

Drain the sauce out of the cooked fish dish into a pot and put over a low heat to simmer. Add cream and mix through until simmering, then turn off the heat and add butter to prevent it splitting.

Prawns

Coat prawns in flour and flash-fry in butter until colour starts to show on both sides.

To serve

Place whole trout onto a serving dish. Spread potatoes and prawns evenly around the dish. Pour butter sauce over the top.

23

THE ROCK

LOCATION
NIUE

✕

FISH OF THE DAY
MAHIMAHI

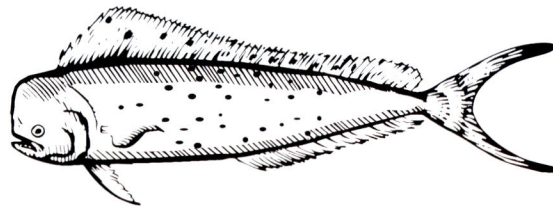

Asking me to choose a favourite Pacific Island is like being asked to pick a favourite child. It's hard, but deep down, secretly, you do have one. It's something that I won't admit publicly for fear of upsetting the others, so let's change the subject and talk about Niue!

Locals call it 'The Rock'. With no outlying islands or reef, it really is just that: a lone coral atoll atop a long-extinct volcano that popped up like a pimple in between the Cook Islands, Samoa and Tonga, situated on the edge of one of the world's deepest trenches. It is one of the most isolated islands in the South Pacific, and at 64 km in circumference, with a population of around 1600, Niue can feel almost totally deserted at times. But it is without question one of the most beautiful islands I've visited.

It's also one of the best dive locations in the Pacific. With no rivers or lagoons, there is little sediment run-off, which results in some of the clearest salt water you will find on the planet. I've had days diving where the visibility has been 60 m or more. For perspective, in New Zealand 25 m visibility is considered champagne diving.

Previous spread
Snorkelling in the crystal-clear water at Avatele Bay in Niue.

And if you want to talk fish — well, here I have line-caught blue marlin, wahoo, giant trevally, bluefin trevally, barracuda, green jobfish, yellowfin tuna and mahimahi amongst others . And, because the water goes so deep so quickly, some of these have been nabbed just metres from the wharf.

As for the spearfishing, anything you can catch on a rod here is also fair game with the speargun, including marlin. I have shot some of my best wahoo here, as well as delivering a solid bull mahimahi to BJ Rex, the chef at the Falala Fa Café in Alofi.

Of course, if you're not into fishing, there's plenty of other places to see and experience. Here's a canapé tray of my favourites: Anapala Chasm — a short, steep walk down 155 steps into a crack with a cool fresh water pool at the bottom — if you are feeling up for it, take a dive torch with your snorkel gear and swim off into the inky blackness; the Talava Arches, a 30-minute walk ending in an Instagram-ready view; Matapa Chasm, an excellent swimming hole where salt and fresh water mix; and the Palaha Cave. Time your visit for sunset with a low tide and take a bottle of something nice. As the sun dips, it fills the cave with an incredible golden light so stunning and romantic that when I went to film it with my cameraman Mike, we nearly got engaged.

On my last trip to Niue, I was lucky enough to be invited along to witness an island custom I won't ever forget: a special haircutting ceremony marking the coming-of-age of a couple of young boys. Their first-ever haircut is an event that includes the whole village.

Two brothers, Kensei and Khanden, from the Tuapa village, were having a combined celebration. Dad Haydon and mum Felicia had been planning it for over 12 months. It was no small affair — Haydon and Felicia had planted three paddocks of taro in anticipation, and on the day 87 pigs were butchered, as well as countless chickens. There was also plenty of fish and other contributed goods.

Now, fascinatingly, this isn't for a feast to end all feasts. The food is actually divided up into piles of various sizes. Then each person who attends donates money to the boys' coming-of-age — the funds set aside

for their family's future — and the goods are then divided up depending on how much each person gave. The boys' hair, which has been plaited into many strands, is then cut by family members and special guests called to the stage to help. The boys are adorned with blankets and cash contributions.

It's a big deal — ceremonies like this can raise northward of NZ$80,000. It is best described as a type of community banking, as the boys' parents will be expected to contribute to other haircutting ceremonies in the village before and after. It was a special occasion that I felt honoured to be a part of, and yet another demonstration of just how unique each of our Pacific Island neighbours truly are.

But it is the ocean around this rock outpost that holds the most fascination for me. From July to October, female humpback whales come here to give birth, and males come to sing and find a bit of holiday romance. Niue is one of only a few places in the world where you are allowed to swim with these whales, and I can't recommend this experience highly enough. At 16 m and weighing 36 tonnes or more, there is something incredibly moving about sharing the water with such a sentient being. I've seen tourists burst into tears after encounters, and I get it. Staring into a mother whale's weary eyes while her calf plays nearby, you feel an absolute connection to the struggle for life she has to endure. In peak season (August) the whales can be prolific, and are often parked right out the front of the island's only resort.

There also aren't many places where you can take yourself for a snorkel out over the reef's edge from the shore. It's possible in several locations here in Niue, but the stand-out spot for me is Avatele — pronounced 'Ava-sell-e' — which I consider one of the best snorkelling destinations in the Pacific. In its small bay there are hundreds of species of fish, but brave the current out to the reef drop-off and the place comes alive. It's

As the sun dips, it fills the cave with an incredible golden light so stunning and romantic that when I went to film it with my cameraman Mike, we nearly got engaged.

Opposite above
Whistling my way to a hair-cutting ceremony with a wheelbarrow full of fish.

Opposite below
A magical sunset from the deck of the Matavai Resort in Niue.

'The ocean is absolutely central to Niueans — for food, for our culture, music, arts and livelihoods. And we have to make sure that it's sustainable going forward, otherwise it changes us as a people considerably.'

— CORAL PASISI

also a real sea snake hotspot — and while yes, they are venomous, their placid, gentle nature and tiny mouth means they are never a threat. Just ask Willie Santelli at the nearby Sundays-only Washaway Café. As a kid he used to wear them like a necklace to impress the ladies.

Speaking of Willie, he's one of the only guides who will take you to the mysterious Vaikona Caves. The name translates as 'sour water', and it's a tough walk that involves ropes and climbing, but is well worth the effort. Another local character, Tony Aholima, is also a great guide if you're keen for a night forage in the bush, chasing another island delicacy: the coconut crab. These guys get huge and tasty and, because of the small human population and a ban on their export a few years ago, there are plenty to find. Just head out after any rain and you'll find them on most of the tracks.

We were keen for BJ Rex to cook us his famous mahimahi and coconut crab dish, and our trip into the bush with Tony produced the goods, with a solid 1 kg coconut crab safely in our sack. Now all we needed was the mahimahi to go with it.

We headed out the next morning at dawn to try to catch one on rod and with the spear. We rigged whole dead flying fish in similar style to what we did in Rarotonga. All we had to do was get the baits past the damned yellowfin and marauding wahoo. Yes, the fishing up here is that good!

One yellowfin and two solid wahoo later, one of the reels started screaming again. This time it was the fish we were after. There were a bunch of mahimahi hanging out at one of the island's FADs (fish aggregation devices), rafts of old netting and buoys floating on the surface but attached to the sea floor hundreds of metres below. Mahimahi are incredibly hard fighters, leaping clear of the water and then using their flat bodies to create huge resistance as you try to reel them in. After a

Mahimahi are incredibly hard fighters, leaping clear of the water and then using their flat bodies to create huge resistance as you try to reel them in.

good 20-minute fight, I had my fish in the boat, so I quickly threw on my wetsuit and grabbed my speargun.

Once in the water, I could see there was an array of species hanging around the FAD, including wahoo, rainbow runners and a mixture of smaller baitfish. Then along came the mahimahi. There would have been about 20 of them, skimming in just beneath the surface.

I picked out a solid male and pulled the trigger. As soon as I did, up from the depths came three or four silky sharks. Time to get busy and get my fish to the boat as soon as possible! Fortunately once I had it within a couple of metres of me, the sharks gave up. Job done!

Now all that was needed to make this trip perfect was for me to finally nail my nemesis, the dogtooth tuna, on spear. Along for the ride was the man who had saved me from near death the last time I attempted this and had blacked out, Brendon Pasisi.

Brendon and his sister Coral are two of the stand-out champions of food security and economic prosperity for the Pacific. Chatting with Coral, you get a real sense of someone who is committed to the retention of culture and the significance of ocean ecosystems and fish as the primary protein source in all the Pacific's cultures. 'A healthy fishery is absolutely critical to the people of Niue,' Coral says. 'The ocean in general is absolutely central to Niueans — for food, for our culture, music, arts and livelihoods. And we have to make sure that it's sustainable going forward, otherwise it changes us as a people considerably.'

Previous spread
The visiting yacht anchorage along the foreshore of Alofi in Niue. Humpbacks are often seen playing in among the boats.

Opposite above
As night descends, the local fruit bats wake up and take flight in search of food.

Opposite below
Niue is the first country in the world to be declared a dark sky nation.

Coral is an earth scientist who is devotedly focused on sustainable development in the Pacific. From the work she does for the Niue Government to her roles on SPREP (Secretariat of the Pacific Regional Environment Programme), PIFS (Pacific Islands Forum Secretariat) and GFC (Global Climate Fund), among others, Coral is the quiet environmental achiever that we all aspire to be.

In pursuit of the dogtooth, Brendon and I headed up the coast before dawn to set up a burley trail, to raise a couple up within range. Finally I had one in my sights, and 25 m down, I got my shot. Of course, the first thing a dogtooth does when it's been speared is head straight for the reef to try to rub the spear off. And by the time I hit the surface and began hauling it off the bottom, the tax men had arrived. Three grey reef sharks chased my fish down, and one managed to latch on before I could pull the dogtooth free. Luckily, I was able to get hold of it before the whole fish got eaten, and with absolute elation I landed my first speared dogtooth. After all the near misses, near death and not-good-enough attempts, I had come to truly appreciate why this fish is considered the ultimate spearfishing target. As a tuna, with its delicious white flesh, absolutely none of it was wasted. In fact, I'm sure the extra effort required made it taste that much better. Now I had just one last bucket-list fish to go: that elusive double-figure trout.

Sitting watching whales in the sunset, cocktail in hand, swapping stories with other tourists while eating incredible fresh fish, my Niue experience was complete. So is Niue my favourite child? Deep down, secretly — well, next time we're allowed to travel you should check it out and make your own decision. I couldn't possibly say.

Opposite page
Finally I get my nemesis, the dogtooth tuna, almost exactly where I nearly drowned trying to do so years before.

STEAMED MAHIMAHI WITH COCONUT RICE AND TEMPURA CRAB

BJ REX, FALALA FA CAFÉ
SERVES 4

Taro chips

1 medium-sized taro,
  julienned for deep-frying
oil for deep-frying

Tempura crab

1 coconut crab
2 egg yolks
300 ml sparkling ice-cold
  water
150 g plain flour
150 g cornflour
salt, to season
oil for frying

Coconut rice

2 cups medium-grain rice
salt
1½ cups coconut cream
grated coconut

Bok choy

bok choy
fresh ginger root

Fish

4 tablespoons light soy
  sauce
2 tablespoons sesame oil
spring onion
fresh ginger root
½ kg mahimahi fillets
peanut oil

Taro chips

Thinly slice the end of a taro into chips, and deep-fry until crisp.

Tempura crab

Boil crab until nearly but not quite cooked through. Allow to drain and stand before shelling and picking the crab meat, trying to keep pieces whole.

Add the egg yolks to the sparkling water and beat until light and fluffy. Add the flour and cornflour and mix together with salt to taste. Do not over beat the mixture.

Batter pieces of crab with tempura mix, and deep- or shallow-fry until crisp.

Coconut rice

Bring the rice to the boil in a pot of water and season with salt. When the rice is almost cooked, add 1½ cups coconut cream and finish with grated coconut for texture. The rice should be moist and firm.

Bok choy

Cut the bok choy in half and put into a hot pan with a little bit of water and chopped ginger. Simmer until cooked through.

Fish

Mix the light soy sauce and sesame oil together in a bowl. Thinly slice the spring onion lengthways, into strips 5–8 cm in length. Slice half the fresh ginger into matching strips, but cut a few wider pieces to add to the fish as it cooks.

Cut the mahimahi into serving-sized pieces. Add a thin layer of water to a deep-dish pan with a lid, or an electric fry pan with a lid, and bring to a simmer. Use the bok choy leaves to create a base for the fish to sit on, elevated just above the water. This is so the fish is steamed and not boiled.

Place the fish on the bed of bok choy in the pan, and put the wider-sliced ginger on top of the fish. Put the lid over the pan to lightly steam the fish — you don't want to cook it all the way through.

Take off the lid and remove the fish just before it is completely cooked.

Remove the ginger and place the par-cooked fish onto a plate. Place the thinly sliced spring onion and thinly sliced fresh ginger on top.

Using a spoon, ladle ¾ of the mixed soy sauce and sesame oil across the top of the fish, ginger and spring onion. Put half a cup of peanut oil into a separate pan over a high heat.

Carefully pour the hot peanut oil across the top of the fish, ginger and spring onion to complete the cooking process.

Add the last of the soy/sesame mix after this.

To serve

Press servings of cooked coconut rice into a small bowl and tip out carefully onto each serving plate, so that it retains its shape.

Add the cooked bok choy to the top of the rice, and place a piece of fish with its ginger and spring onion topping onto the bok choy.

Sprinkle taro chips around each plate, and cut the tempura crab pieces in half before adding on top of the fish to complete the dish.

24

THE LADY

LOCATION
TAHITI

X

FISH OF THE DAY
PAPIO

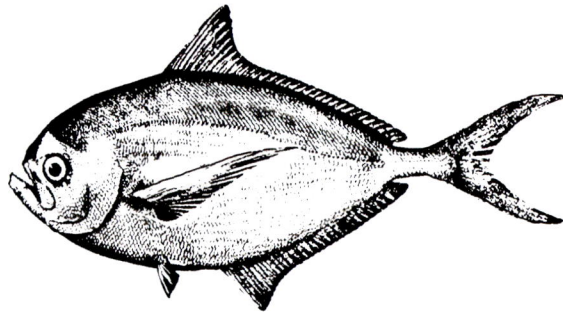

Of the 118 islands that make up French Polynesia, scattered across 5 million sq km of the South Pacific Ocean, Tahiti is where we all begin our journey of discovery — unless, of course, you have arrived by boat. The home of Polynesian peoples for more than 2000 years, from the earliest days of Pacific voyaging by Europeans, Tahiti gained a name for itself as a welcoming refuge for visiting sailors — a tropical paradise bountiful in produce, combined with the local people's liberal attitude to sex. It was little wonder that it became the scene of multiple desertions and mutinies. One ship even reportedly started falling apart after the nails that held it together became a valuable commodity in the trade for 'favours' with local women. Both Britain and France wanted it for themselves, and the French eventually made it a colony in 1880.

Tahiti is made up of two islands connected at one narrow point, known as Tahiti-Nui and Tahiti-Iti , 'nui' meaning big and 'iti' meaning small. These names are a good example of the strong ties that New Zealand has to this place — the words have the same meanings in te reo Māori.

Previous spread
An outrigger canoe powers through the clear waters of Moorea, Tahiti.

Captain James Cook's success in communicating with Māori when he arrived in New Zealand was attributed to his Tahitian navigator Tupaia who, thanks to the similarities in language, could converse freely with his New Zealand cousins. It is also a clear demonstration of the Tahitians' superior ocean-navigation skills, as it is believed that regular trips were made back and forth from these islands to New Zealand, many hundreds of years before Cook's arrival.

I was curious to discover if there was another side to the Tahiti touted by glossy brochures — home to the most beautiful people on the planet. Were they living the dream along coasts dotted with perfect white-sand beaches, framed by towering, jungle-clad mountains? So the first thing I did on arrival was head out of downtown Pape'ete and across to the Tahiti-iti side of the island, arriving at a homestay next to a village called Teahupo'o. Pronounced 'Chi-ow-poo', it's home to one of the most famous surf breaks in the world.

Charles Darwin used Moorea to establish his theory of the formation of coral atolls, but my own theory is that the island could be the origin of the term 'island time', with life unwinding at very much its own pace.

As luck would have it, the World Surfing League was on during our visit (pre-Covid, of course), and there was a huge swell running. Even for non-surfers the waves here are a spectacle, as raw ocean comes rolling straight in and dumps over a steeply angled reef. Although the break is offshore, local boats are keen to take surfers and sightseers alike out to witness the action. It's possible to get so close that barrelling waves will spit sea mist into your face as you watch from just metres away.

It was good also to get away from the fancy resorts and try out Tahiti's tourist homestay system. Typically, a family home will have one or two adjoining properties that are completely self-sufficient, often set in prime position on the water's edge. My welcoming homestay owner Poerani Durand's guesthouses felt almost Balinese, with large mosquito nets

draped above four-poster beds. There was also a private open-plan outdoor communal area, which looked over a small pool out to the expansive lagoon beyond. Poe invited us to the main house one evening, where she showed me a local Tahitian raw fish speciality using yellowfin tuna.

This type of accommodation is considerably cheaper than any of the resorts, and the food outside of the resorts was also considerably better. Dotted along the roadsides are what the locals call roulettes, which roughly translates as 'food truck'. These are parked-up trucks or caravans set up permanently with seating and a cover out front. Nearly all are family-run, with a great deal of pride put into the menus, and they're a fun place to eat with locals and visitors alike.

When I had asked Thibault how he felt when he was grabbing the trace on a 1000-pounder, 'Terrified' had been his answer, and I could see why.

However, I was here to spend time not on land but at sea, with another lady, one who has a reputation as one of the best in her game. Game fishing, that is. We were lucky enough to have been invited to join the *Ultimate Lady*, a Kiwi-owned, 28 m wave-piercing catamaran with a reputation for catching fish — lots of fish. She once caught 453 marlin all weighing in excess of 200 pounds each in just 50 days!

Her skipper is New Zealand-born Tom Francis, and I would call him a lucky guy. Tom was there for the build of the *Lady* and worked his way onboard, skippering her since 2001, and he's never looked back. It's always nice to have a good boat to fish from, as it certainly improves your chances of hooking up, but when you have the very latest technology and a 28 m fishing machine like no other, things get, well, surreal. And what a place to find yourself fishing for a living. Up here, especially in the Marquesas, granders (fish weighing more than 1000 pounds, or 450 kg) are a regular occurrence, and there is plenty more to chase with rod and reel in the 5 million sq km of Tahiti's exclusive economic zone.

Once we were on board, Tom introduced us to the technology he uses to find and catch more marlin than pretty much any other boat — and what a set-up it was! First, he uses bird radar to locate birds feeding, then gyro-stabilised binoculars to confirm the species. If they are the

Opposite above
Our guide helping me feed a stingray called Moorea.

Opposite below
That iconic South Pacific Instagram shot, sunset through coconut palms, never gets old.

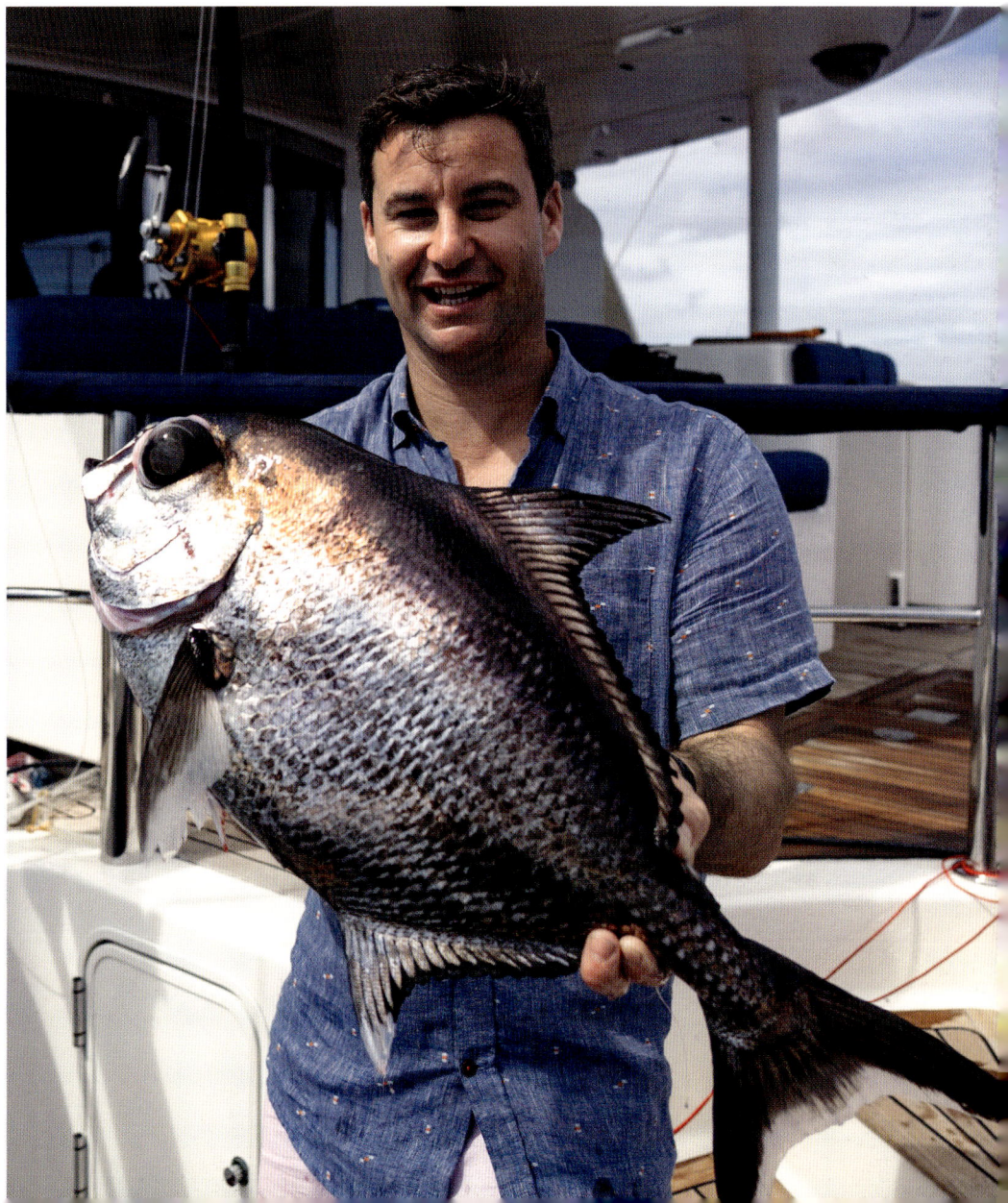

About an hour into our journey, Tom began counting down, 'Three, two, one . . .', and right on cue one of the reels began to howl as a feisty little blue marlin started porpoising away from the boat.

right type of birds, then the hunt is on.

Next up, as they get within 800 m of the action, a sonar post is lowered through one of the hulls, giving Tom 360-degree imagery under the water. With this he can identify individual marlin and track their speed, direction and depth, allowing him to put the lures right across their nose. These fish Tom refers to as 'electronic marlin'.

So, does it work? Well, about an hour into our journey, Tom began counting down from the intercom on the bridge, 'Three, two, one . . .', and right on cue one of the gold Penn reels began to howl as a feisty little blue marlin started porpoising away from the boat. I was on the rod only five minutes before Tom had backed us down on a very green fish, which hadn't been worn down at all by the short fight and was still extremely feisty. Thibault (pronounced Tibo) the deckhand got a wrap on the trace. Then all hell broke loose, as the fish leapt clear out of the water repeatedly as Thibault hung on for dear life. I remembered a conversation I'd had with him the night before when I asked how he felt when he was grabbing the trace on a 1000-pounder. 'Terrified' had been his answer and I could see why — this fish was only about 150 pounds (68 kg) and he had his work cut out just holding on. Finally it calmed down enough to be tagged and released, and on we went.

Next up it was the hunt for a particularly flavoursome deep-water species — the papio or Ray's bream. For this we used another fancy bit of kit — a sounder normally found in deep-water commercial boats that could give accurate biomass and individual animal sizes at more than 1 km down. A couple of drifts and we had our bream, as well as a sizeable Peruvian oilfish.

Both these fish are considered delicacies here in Tahiti, with the latter having a rather explosive side effect — eat too much and within an hour or so, you'll be in the bathroom. It's the ultimate cure for constipation, with the effects lasting a week or more. I couldn't help myself, and wow, is this fish tasty. Actually, it's a bit *too* tasty and I made the fatal mistake of

having 'just a bit more', which tipped me over the edge. I'll spare you the details, but suffice it to say that the oilfish's 'other' reputation is very well deserved.

Our journey on the *Lady* took us to another island, one regularly described as the most beautiful in the world. There are plenty of islands with similar features, so what earns a place that specific honour? What sets it apart and gives it that edge? Is it the angular nature of the mountains that rise out of the sea, with razor-sharp ridgelines of impossible steepness overlapping into the distance like a page of drop-shadowed fonts? Perhaps it's the perfect combination of colours: deep azure water outside the perfect curves of reef, accentuated by the white breaking waves and long yellow-sand beaches circling an island painted with the deep green hue only a tropical rainforest can emanate. Or perhaps it's simply the people, warmly embracing visitors young and old.

Compared to busy Tahiti, the pageant-winning Moorea feels so much further away from home in terms of pace and lifestyle. Charles Darwin used the island to establish his theory of the formation of coral atolls, but my own theory is that the island could be the origin of the term 'island time', with life unwinding at very much its own pace. I can absolutely see what Darwin saw in this place — it must have felt a world away from his experience of the rough whalers and sealers he met in New Zealand's Bay of Islands.

To keep you busy while you relax, inland Moorea has everything from hiking to zip-lining, while on the water you can go swimming and sightseeing with whales and sharks. And no trip to Moorea can be considered complete without a swim with the friendly local stingrays, a social-media-picture staple and fantastic chance to get up close to a bit of nature. Local guides have trained these underwater car bonnets to glide in and accept offerings of fish right from your hands.

In what seemed like just a few hours, our week's journey through these islands came to an end — but not without a few conversations with Tom about our return.

'Marquesas, Tom?'

'Absolutely, mate — let's get a plan together.'

Fingers crossed it won't be long before that one.

Previous spread
My blue marlin goes crazy off the back of the boat while deckhand Thibault hangs on to the trace.

CHARCOAL PAPIO

MICHAEL MU SAN
SERVES 4

Salad
1 romaine lettuce
½ kg baby tomatoes
½ red onion
2 spring onions
100 g goat's cheese
olive oil
lemon wedges, to serve

Coconut rice
1 cup of long-grain rice
100 g desiccated coconut
1 cup of coconut cream

Fish
½ kg papio or similar
  dense deep-sea fish
clarified butter or light oil
salt and pepper

Fire up a charcoal barbecue. Wait till the fire burns down to consistent red coals.

Make a rough salad from ingredients and toss in a generous splash of olive oil.

Cook rice and add desiccated coconut and coconut cream to just cover, not soak.

Cut the papio into even 1 cm thick slices. Coat with clarified butter, season with salt and pepper and place on barbecue. Cook till white colour is one-third of the way through the fish and turn. Cook till other side is one-third cooked and rest. The fish should cook through while resting.

Plating instructions
Plate up side salad and rice and serve with a wedge of lemon.

25

THE CLUB

LOCATION
CHRISTCHURCH TO
TEKAPO, NEW ZEALAND

FISH OF THE DAY
SALMON

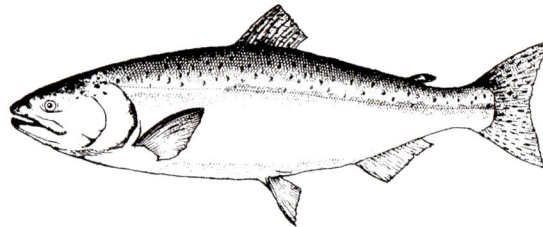

I had a plan. For five long years I had chased a rite of passage, trying to get my mythical membership into the exclusive double-figure club by catching a trout weighing over 10 pounds (4.5 kg), to no avail. I came close in Wanaka, missed in Taupō, and got even closer in Rotorua, but still that double-figure trout eluded me.

On this trip I was in Christchurch to catch up with world-renowned dolphin expert Dr Liz Slooten, to find out how one of our most endangered indigenous dolphins, Hector's dolphin, was doing. Liz has devoted many years to researching the dolphin, and had some sad news.

'The main cause of death is fishing, without any shadow of a doubt,' she tells me. 'And that's not the kind of fishing that you or I do — if people went out there only with their speargun or their hook and line or their fishing rod there would be no problem whatsoever. But if you want to use these bulk-fishing methods like gillnetting and trawling, then you're going to be catching dolphins.'

Today, estimates are that there are only between 10,000 and 15,000 of these cute little mammals left, less than half the population when Liz first started studying them. The latest NIWA estimate is that during the years 2000–06, between 110 and 150 of these dolphins were killed *each year* in fishing nets. Let that sink in. This is why commercial fishing around their habitats is already limited, but Liz believes it's not limited enough to save the species. When the conversation turns to the Hector's cousin the Māui dolphin, the population of which is down to approximately 60 animals, her tone sinks further. 'I'm not against fishing — we just need to get fishing methods that catch dolphins removed from all areas that these cetaceans call home.'

While I was in the south, I thought it was a great opportunity to go fishing for salmon and trout in the hydro canals of the Mackenzie Basin. The timing was perfect: it was winter and therefore spawning season in the canals.

The South Island's hydroelectricity canal systems are nothing short of an engineering work of art. The sheer scale of the river and lake diversions is hard to get your head around at first. A number of man-made water races funnel melted glacial snow down chutes kilometres long to giant turbine generators. What's even more impressive is that the potential of the area for electricity generation was recognised way back in 1904, even though the creation of the canal system was not started until the 1920s, and the project not completed until the 1980s. The result is enough clean power to light up and heat more than 800,000 homes.

Today, the Tekapo district provides a platform for all sorts of extracurricular pursuits, from boating, hiking, biking, skiing and, of course, fishing. Being high in the mountains also means the air is incredibly clean and clear, resulting in the night skies above Tekapo being declared a Dark Sky Sanctuary back in 2012. Strict rules are now in place, so extraneous light such as from streetlights is minimised, to enable people to crane their necks and marvel at the darkness above, littered with a milky sea of stars and planets — a view obscured in almost every urban area in the world. To experience this in person is to stir feelings of your place in the universe, and I can't help but wonder if people

Following spread
One of Canterbury's most polluted bodies of water — Te Waihora or Lake Ellesmere.

'I'm not against fishing — we just need to get fishing methods that catch dolphins removed from all areas that these cetaceans call home.'

— DR LIZ SLOOTEN, DOLPHIN RESEARCHER

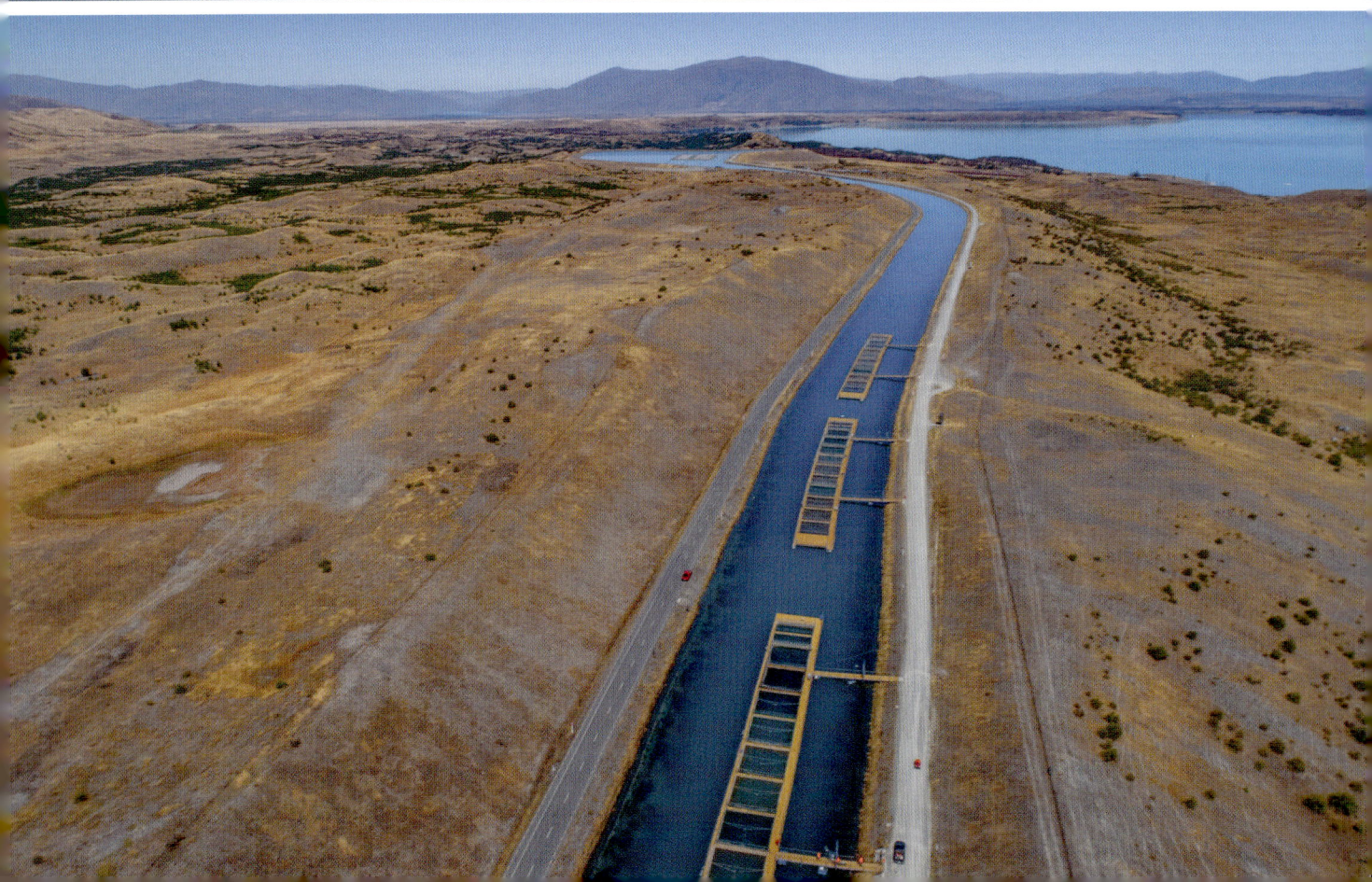

Moon cycles are known to trigger bite-times, approaching weather systems can encourage nibbles, a butterfly flapping its wings deep in a Fiordland valley can signal a feeding session. It's all quite mysterious, but when it's on, it's on.

might think differently about life itself if more of them could glimpse their own insignificance demonstrated here from above.

Below this celestial mosaic, the diverted hydro water has gently drifted its milky way downstream for decades, creating nothing but clean power. Until some bright spark one day thought to themselves, 'Hmmm, I wonder if we could use that water for something else?' From this came the salmon farms, cages anchored inside the canals where fat fish flourish and occasionally escape. Then around these farms were released the even chubbier trout, although I suspect they had found a way to introduce themselves much earlier, so good are they at populating New Zealand river systems.

The result? Well, as one keen Australian angler I met on the banks told me, 'Where else in the world would they let you do this? Where in the world would they not only let you come and fish a waterway that is a power supply for a country, but also farm in it?'

This was a resource that not only supplied energy but grew highly sought-after freshwater salmon for export and also brought millions of dollars in extra revenue into the district through fishing tourism. The campervans parked up and down one causeway I visited, the canal edge lined with happy visitors all casting a line, was testament to this.

Not only are there both salmon and trout to catch, and plenty of them, but these waterways also produce some of the largest trout in the world. Fish have been pulled from here that wouldn't look out of place as a character in a Marvel film. They're so mind-bendingly large that they look more like professional wrestlers than fish. Have a go at absorbing this: the current pending world-record brown trout was caught in one of these canals, and weighed in at 55 pounds or 24.9 kg. This is a trout we're talking about. I mean, even a 25 kg kingfish is a mountable fish, but a

Opposite above
Fishermen line the edge of the Tekapo Canal power station pool with Aoraki/Mount Cook in the background.

Opposite below
The Aoraki salmon farm in the Tekapo Canal system.

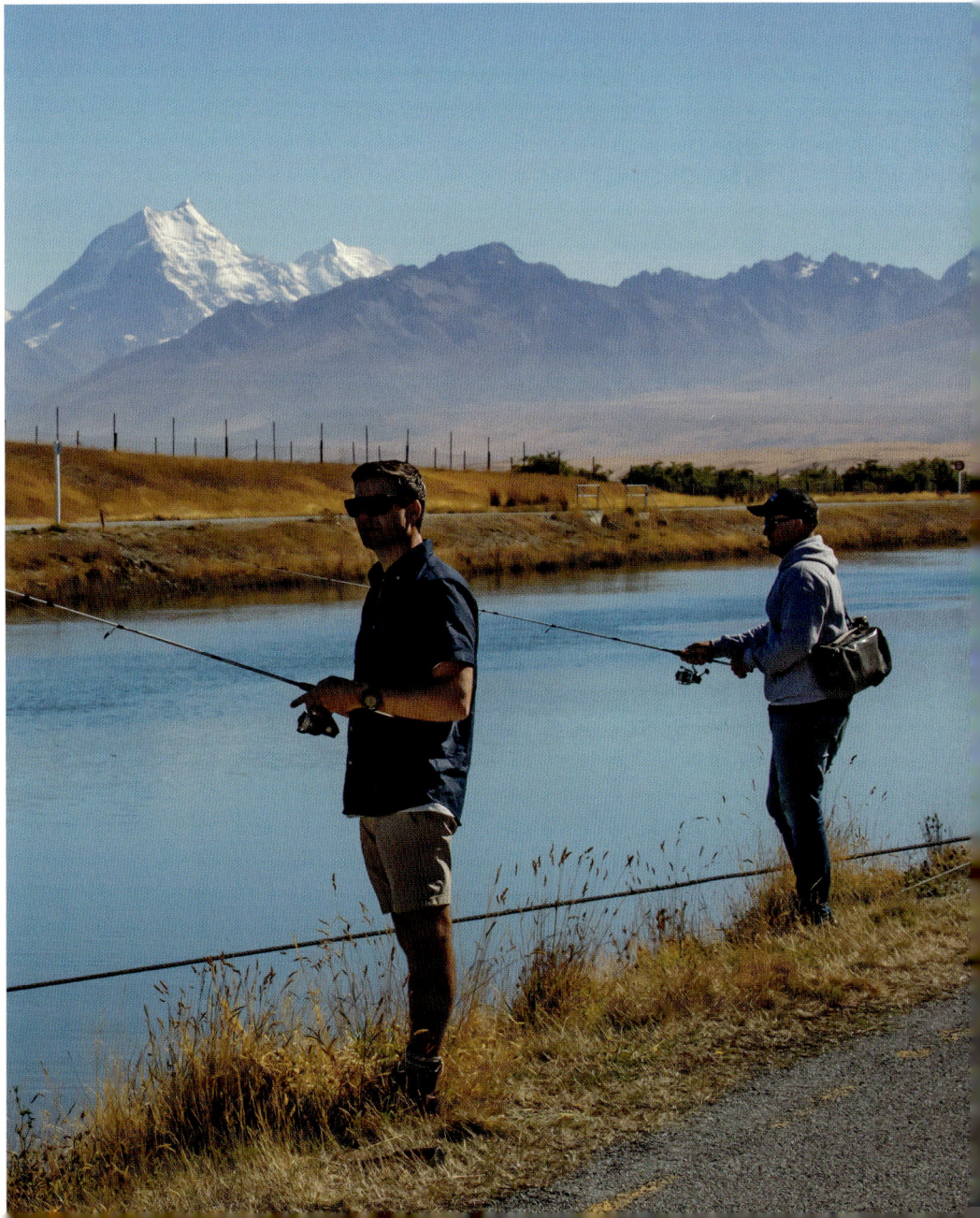

> **The trout basically plonk themselves in a bit of a hole, open their mouths and sit there while the current sends snacks downstream to fill their chubby cheeks.**

trout? Come on, now — that is outrageous!

For a long time, people assumed that the trout here have grown to these ginormous dimensions by feeding off the pellets being fed to the fish at the nearby salmon farms. However, scientists did some tests, including studying a whole section of canal that was drained for repair, to learn that that's not necessarily the case at all. It turns out that because the races never flood — their water levels are always controlled by the power companies — the weed bed within them is able to flourish, creating a perfect habitat for small fish and other trout-food sources to thrive. The trout then basically plonk themselves in a bit of a hole, open their mouths and sit there while the current sends snacks downstream to fill their chubby cheeks.

The downside of this is that they can be notoriously tricky to catch. They're arguably the fussiest freshwater fish on the planet! Moon cycles are known to trigger bite-times, approaching weather systems can encourage nibbles, a butterfly flapping its wings deep in a Fiordland valley can signal a feeding session. It's all quite mysterious, but when it's on, it's on.

One very good bite-trigger is increased flow in the canals as demand for electricity goes up — demand such as people getting up and putting the kettle on and making breakfast. So it is not an exaggeration to suggest that someone in Auckland making toast and a cup of tea might well be contributing to a world-record trout catch down south. This action might stir the fish into a bit of careless activity that could see it bite at a fisher's lure, cast from the bank in one of the prettiest fishing destinations on the planet.

It was this 'making of toast' that I was up early to take advantage of. I was fishing a method called egg-rolling, using a drifting pretend fish-egg soft bait moving along at the speed of the current, close to the bottom. As the flow picked up to cater to all those morning cups of tea, I was ready to

Previous spread, clockwise from top left
Local fisher Christina with a nice salmon for the table; Fishing the Ohau River on a picture-postcard day; Using the egg-rolling technique to fish for giant trout on the Magic Carpet near Tekapo; Guide Adam Royter fishing the Tekapo Canal with Aoraki/Mount Cook in the background; A spectacular sunset over Lake Tekapo; Surrounding shorelines also support a diverse range of flora.

Opposite page
I finally join the 'double-figure club' with this monster rainbow jack tipping the scales at a whopping 16.1 pounds.

take advantage. And I did. *Finally*, after a huge take, I was hooked up to a fish of a lifetime.

Backwards and forwards I was dragged along the canal bank. Then suddenly came the realisation that I didn't have a landing net (not that I owned one big enough for what was on the end of my line!). However, such is the camaraderie here on the canals that within minutes of me hooking my monster fish a shout came from along the bank: 'Need a net, mate?' Down the bank came a fishing guide, leaving his paying customer to come to the rescue of one very excited stranger. He even supplied guidance on how to land my prize, and once it was in the net supplied the scales to safely weigh it. It ended up tipping those scales at a whopping 16.1 pounds (7.3 kg).

To demonstrate just how good this patch of water really is, I managed to follow up by netting and releasing a second monster of over 12 pounds (5.4 kg), all before lunchtime. Oh, and I got a nice fat salmon to add to my bag.

Like conquering my nemesis the dogtooth tuna both on rod and reel and on spear, the elation and satisfaction of being able to take a seat in the club of all trout-fishing clubs was well worth all the heartache and frustration along the way. In fact, my earlier disappointments only made this success feel that much better. And, in a nutshell, that is the attraction, and addiction, to fishing.

NORI-CRUSTED WILD SALMON ON AN ESCABECHE OF PICKLED VEGETABLES

JAMES DRAPER
SERVES 4

4 x 170 g salmon portions, skin off
12 Bluff oysters (keep oyster water for sauce)
12 fresh greenlip mussels

Escabeche

1 fennel bulb, julienned
1 red capsicum, julienned
1 yellow capsicum, julienned
1 courgette, julienned
1 onion, julienned
olive oil
200 ml sherry vinegar
salt and pepper

Nori crumb

3 sheets unseasoned nori
20 g white sesame seeds

Champagne sauce

2 shallots, finely diced
50 ml clarified butter
300 ml champagne or good-quality sparkling wine
50 ml oyster water, strained (from above)
50 ml mussel juices, strained (from steamed mussels)
200 ml cream

Garnish

ice plant, beach spinach and chervil

Escabeche

Slice the vegetables and set aside. Heat the olive oil in a saucepan to a moderate heat, add the vegetables and cook for 3 minutes without colouring. Deglaze with sherry vinegar and cook for a further 2 minutes, then season with salt and pepper.

Nori crumb

Place nori and sesame seeds in food processor. Blend until fine, scraping sides occasionally. Season, then place on a plate and press the salmon pieces skin-side down into the nori crumb. Set aside.

Mussels

Steam the mussels in a cup of water. As soon as they open, remove from water, shell, remove beards and set aside.

Champagne sauce

Sweat the shallots in the clarified butter until soft but without colour. Deglaze with champagne and reduce by half. Add the strained oyster water, mussel juices and cream, and reduce to sauce consistency. Check seasoning and keep warm.

Cooking

Preheat the oven to 170°C. Heat a non-stick frying pan over a moderate heat and add some olive oil. Once hot, carefully add seasoned salmon fillets, nori side down, lightly pressing down to ensure the nori is getting crispy. Once crispy, place in the oven for around 5 minutes (depending on how you like your salmon cooked — 5 minutes will yield a medium piece of salmon).

While the salmon is cooking, gently heat the escabeche of vegetables, and in a separate pan heat the champagne sauce. When the salmon is almost cooked, gently place the oysters and mussels into the champagne sauce, just to warm through. Once warm, remove from the sauce. Use a stick blender to blend the sauce.

To serve

Place some warmed escabeche of vegetables in the middle of each plate. Place some cooked salmon on top and arrange some oysters and cooked mussels around the dish. Froth up the champagne sauce with the stick blender and spoon over the oysters and salmon. Garnish with sea herbs.

INDEX OF FISH

Opposite page
With a humpback and her calf in the clear waters of Niue.

RECIPE INDEX

The recipes featured in this book were designed by some of the best chefs in New Zealand and the Pacific. While the recipes focus on the species caught in each episode, other types of seafood can easily be used. To give some guidance, we have categorised them into five main groups: those requiring mild white-fleshed fish, those requiring stronger-flavoured or oily fish, those requiring game fish such as tuna, those requiring freshwater fish, and those requiring cephalopods, shellfish and crustaceans.

Remember: Always pay attention to where your fish has come from and whether it was harvested sustainably. By trying the lesser known types of fish, you can help reduce pressure on fish stocks that might be struggling from overfishing. If using reef fish from the Pacific, check with local fishers as many species contain the poison ciguatera and this varies from location to location.

ABOUT THE AUTHORS

Mike Bhana is a celebrated documentary director, cameraman and writer dedicated to the ocean and ocean conservation. During his 23 years in the television industry, he has produced, directed and shot over 60 hours of natural history documentaries and prime-time material for channels like Discovery, Animal Planet and National Geographic, including 28 films specifically about sharks. His documentary work has resulted in more than a dozen international awards for excellence. While he has a special love of the ocean, Mike has also travelled the world with the Red Cross, documenting the work of its teams in some of the most dangerous and stricken areas of the planet, and more recently co-founded Sea Aid, a not-for-profit organisation aimed at supporting the Pacific Islands achieve better health outcomes. Mike lives on the Coromandel Peninsula with his family, where he has been known to effortlessly whip out a kingie and a couple of crayfish before breakfast (sustainably of course). That's if the surf isn't calling.

Clarke Gayford knew he wanted to be a fisherman before he was 10 years old and had memorised all the Latin, Māori and English names of the fish found along the Gisborne/Mahia coastline he called his backyard. In a 20-year career as a successful television and radio host, Clarke created the cult-status Otago University student television chronicle *Cow TV* and fronted a variety of high-profile travel, entertainment and music shows before responding to the call of the sea and quite literally diving back into it in his late 30s to front *Fish of the Day*. An active advocate of 'spare fishing' over 'spear fishing', Clarke is passionate about connecting people to the ocean. He is the partner of New Zealand Prime Minister Jacinda Ardern, father to daughter Neve, and lives in Auckland.

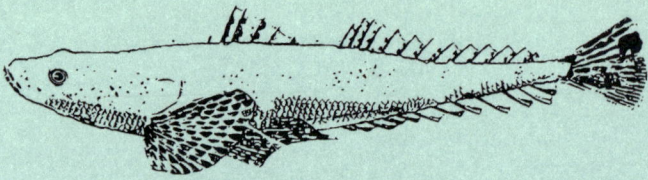

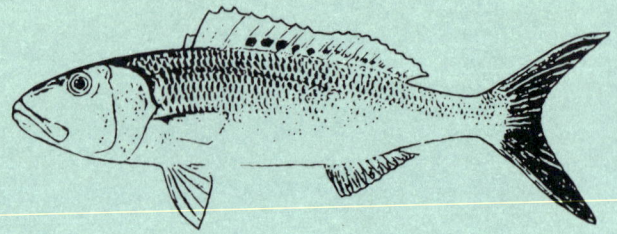

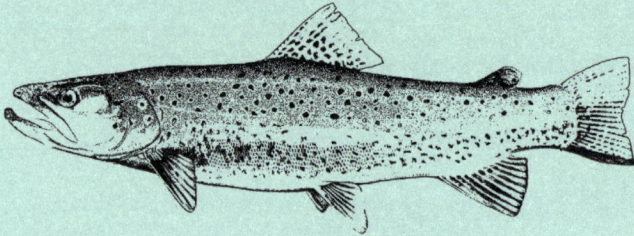

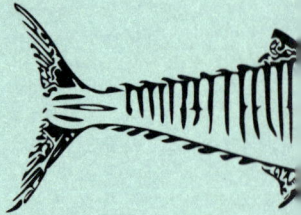

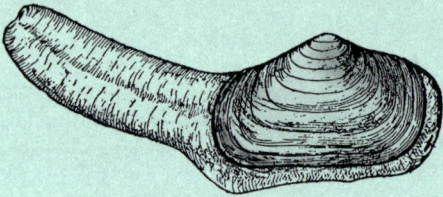

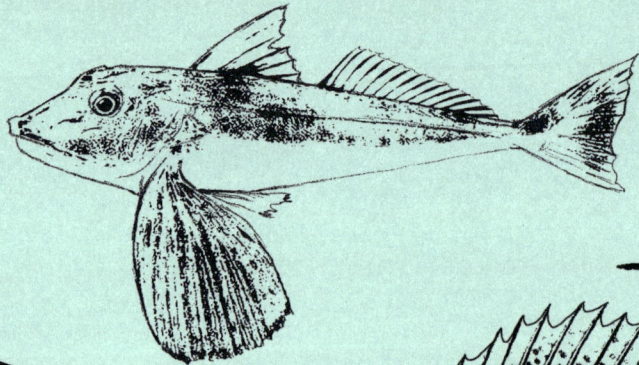

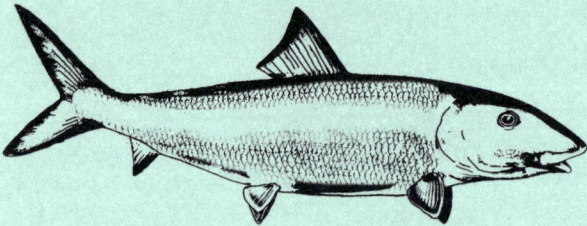

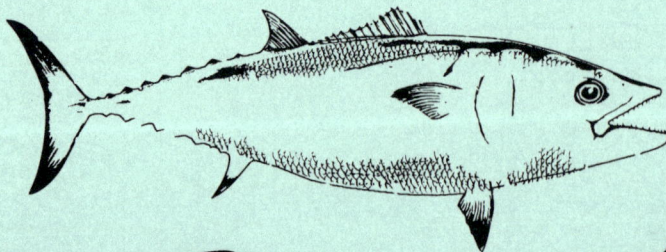

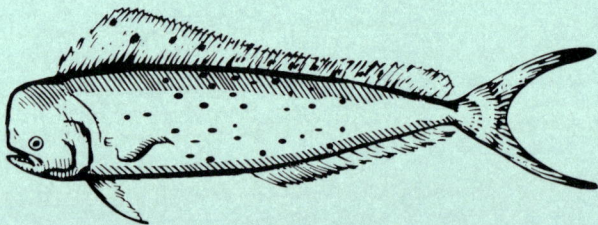